Informatics In Europe

Preparing for the Global Market

Henry Norton

NCC Blackwell

MANCHESTER • OXFORD

British Library Cataloguing in Publication Data

Norton, H
  Informatics in Europe : Preparing for the global market
  1. Information services 2. Europe.
  I. Title
  025.52094

ISBN 1-85554-000-2

© NCC BLACKWELL, 1991

First published in 1991 by:

NCC Blackwell Limited, 108 Cowley Road, Oxford OX4 1JF, England.

Editorial Office: The National Computing Centre Limited, Oxford Road, Manchester M1 7ED, England.

Typeset in 11/13pt Palacio by M Wilson, The National Computing Centre Limited; and printed by Hobbs the Printers of Southampton.

ISBN 1-85554-000-2

Contents

Page

Acknowledgements

Introduction

1 The European Community   1

Introduction   1
Formation and development of the community   1
Decision making in the community   2
The Single European Act   5
Implications of the Single Market   10
Other Community initiatives   12
External relationships   15
Directorate General XIII   19

2 The Informatics Industry   21

Introduction   21
Improvement of the European informatics
   industry   21
Reasons for progress   24
The need to sustain effort   24
Semiconductors   25
Software   27
Telecommunications   27
The skills shortage   30
The elements for success   32

3 Industrial Competitiveness and Strategies   35

Introduction   35
Developing a European strategy   37
Marketing   43
Electronic Data Interchange (EDI)   45
SPRINT   50
Technology innovation information   55
BC-NET   59

4 Collaborative Programmes in Research and Development   61

Introduction   61
The Framework programme   61
The ESPRIT programme   67
RACE   74
AIM   80
DRIVE   81
COST   82
EUREKA   83
PROTEAS   84
Preparation of proposals   85

5 Collaborative Programmes in Education and Training   87

Introduction   87
EUROTECNET II   88
COMETT   91
DELTA   97
ERASMUS   100
LINGUA   101
EUROTRA   103
Other Programmes   103

6 Standards and Open Systems   105

Introduction   105
Informatics Standards   107
European directives   109
Accreditation and certification   112
Open systems   113

The OSI reference model 117
Other OSI standards 120
Implementation of open systems 122
COSINE 123
RARE 125
SPAG 126
Effect on European industry 127
Other addresses 128

7 Legislation 129

Introduction 129
Computer fraud 131
Computer forgery 132
Damage to computer data or computer programs 132
Unauthorised access 133
Unauthorised interception 135
Unauthorised reproduction of a protected
   computer program 135
Unauthorised reproduction of a topography 141
An optional list of computer crimes 142
Data protection 144
Directive on Visual Display Units 145

8 Professionalism 147

Introduction 147
Professional qualifications across Europe 149
The professional challenges 151
The professional society in Europe 153

Glossary 155

Bibliography 163

Index 165

Acknowledgements

Much of the material contained in this book has been collated from articles in 'IT in Europe' and I gratefully acknowledge the permission of A Plus Publications to reproduce the copyright material. It would have been too cumbersome to acknowledge authorship of each paragraph that has been quoted, even though in many cases I have not presumed to change the wording used by the experts. The authors and their organisations are quoted as follows:

C Arnall of KPMG Peat Marwick McLintock
K Bartlett of Department of Trade and Industry
J Bogod of the British Standards Institution
S Coggins of Amdahl International Management Services Ltd
R Cooper, UK Universities and Research Councils and a member of the RARE Executive Committee
R E Dibble of Central Computer and Telecommunications Agency
J Drew of Offices of the Commission of the European Communities
M Duhamel of the European Association for the Transfer of Technologies, Innovation and Industrial Information
J A Elmore of STC Communications
B Gibbens of SEMA
B B Goodman of the Commission of the European Communities
J Harris of the Cabinet Office
J Hobday of the Department of Trade and Industry, UK
N Howell of Technology Marketing Europe
J Ivinson of John Ivinson & Associates Ltd
F Jordan of Policy and Programmes Division, Training Agency

M Kahn of the University of London
A H Kent of the University of London
T Lawrence of 'IT in Europe' (Brussels)
B Oakley of Logica, Cambridge Ltd
A Osborn of the Article Numbering Association (UK) Ltd
N Roberts of International Network Services Ltd
G Smith and C Millard of Clifford Chance (Solicitors)
T Wilkinson of 'IT in Europe'
R Wilmot of OASIS Ltd
J Wishney of Electronic Data Systems.

Introduction

The term *'informatics'* is becoming widely used throughout Europe to mean the application of computers and data-communications to process, store and transmit information, in numeric, text or graphic form. The term *'information technology'* implies an emphasis on the technology or the mechanisms used to deal with the information. Most users are concerned with what is being done rather than with how it is being done. Since this book is concerned with the use of technology as a tool for management, research and education, the term informatics is more appropriate.

Many of the topics covered in this book are aimed at using informatics to improve the competitiveness of European companies in world markets and would be relevant even if there were no progress to a single European market. The advent of the Single Market adds impetus to the need for European companies to make best use of informatics to improve their effectiveness. In the first place, the home market in each member state will be open to suppliers throughout the Community and it will no longer be possible for indigenous companies to have a favoured and secure position. Conversely, progressive companies will be able to extend their marketing and sales throughout Europe, thereby gaining economies of scale in production, thus increasing their profits.

Many American and Japanese companies have been quick to realise the opportunities opened up by a single European community of 323,165,000 people and are developing strategies to exploit the consumer market. It is one of the largest in the world — the populations of the USA and Japan are, respectively, 247,732,000 and 122,783,000. Moreover, discussions are taking place that may extend the European market to the six EFTA countries, which will increase the consumer population by another 31,908,000 people. Trade between the Community and Eastern Europe seems likely to increase, although there are still many restrictions to be overcome. Nevertheless, the opportunities for European trade are continually expanding.

If any European company fails to take advantage of the opportunities offered by the Single Market then others, both within Europe and elsewhere, will.

So what should managers do to ensure that their company achieves the benfits?

The first requirement is to find out what is going on. A great deal of information is available about the activities aimed at developing common legislation and technical standards, collaborative programmes in research and education, open procurement procedures and mutual recognition of professional qualifications. The main aim of this book is to collate such information.

Secondly, companies should find out how decisions are made and influence those decisions so that their problems and interests can be taken into account. In the definition and adoption of technical standards, for example, there is sometimes a conflict of interest between users and vendors. Users should, therefore, get involved in the making of those standards.

In working to influence decisions, it is advisable to collaborate with other companies. Representations from groups of companies or organisations have more effect than individual submissions. Moreover, the effectiveness can be increased by involvement with groups of companies or trade associations from several countries, particularly if their recommendations are European rather than national.

Finally, organisations will need to redefine their business strategies — continually. The rapid pace of technological change would make this necessary in any case. The rapid progress to global trade, which is being accelerated by the formation of the European market, reinforces this need.

INTRODUCTION

The main requirement is to reorganise so that decisions can be made more quickly and so that these decisions can be more innovative. One way, in many cases the only way, to provide the comprehensive up-to-date information needed for these decisions is through informatics.

Robb Wilmot, Founder and Chairman of OASIS (Organisation and Systems Innovations Ltd), recommends that a model of the organisation as an information system should be constructed with managers represented as information processors and new informatics systems represented as new behaviour. The whole structure of the organisation should be overhauled to reduce the hierarchy and remove departmental barriers so that decisions can be made rapidly by the most appropriate person, taking into account the implications for the whole organisation.

Relationships with customers and suppliers should be reviewed. The use of electronic data interchange (EDI), for example, makes it possible to improve the speed with which orders are placed, products are distributed and invoices are submitted. Efficiency can thereby be enhanced, especially when trading on an international scale.

Likewise, relationships with other organisations working in the same area need to be considered. Mergers and acquisitions are drastic steps, but have been effective in some instances. CAP was founded as a European company in 1962 and floated on the London Stock Exchange in 1975. The European branch was taken over by the French partners and renamed CAP-Gemini-Sogeti (CGS) and is now the largest software house in Europe.

The UK branch of CAP merged with the French systems house Sema-Metra in 1988. Initially there were problems, mainly cultural, but none have been insuperable and the resulting company, SEMA is now very successful.

There are many forms of collaboration with peer organisations. The various programmes described in Chapters 4 and 5 provide opportunities for sharing, experience and resources for research and development, training and education. In many cases, co-operation on these projects has been carried forward to commercial collaboration in production and marketing.

Marketing offers many options for collaboration. Practices accepted as the normal way of doing business in one country may be incomprehensible to someone from another country. There are advantages, therefore, in employing a local firm to market goods or tender for work in another member state. Conversely, of course, it may be possible to help a company from another member state market its goods or tender for work in the home country. This applies particularly in bidding for government or local authority contracts where the procedures are often prescribed and involve detailed knowledge of accepted local practices.

I have tried to write from the 'European' viewpoint as I believe that informatics transcends national boundaries, and it is only by working with people throughout Europe that it will be possible to compete with international companies based in America or Japan. This applies not only to companies supplying informatics equiment and services but to those that use informatics — which includes most sectors of industry and commerce. Nevertheless, since my experience is mainly in the UK, it is inevitable that the examples and implications have a UK bias. Readers in other member states should be able to extrapolate information which is relevant to their local situation.

Telephone numbers are given in two forms, as appropriate to the UK eg 010 322 235 1111, or to other member states eg +322 235 1111, where the '+' must be replaced by their own international prefix.

It is virtually impossible for any one person to be familiar with all the implications of '1992'. Moreover, the scene is changing rapidly — politically and industrially as well as technically.

Nevertheless, this book will serve as a point of reference which can be used to set other, particularly later, developments in context.

Henry Norton
London
July 1990

1 The European Community

INTRODUCTION

This chapter provides the essential background that is needed to understand the references to the European Community policy and programmes and the European Community in general. It covers the structure, how decisions are made; the single European Act; other social and fiscal objectives and the Directorate General responsible for Telecommunications, Information Industries and Innovation.

FORMATION AND DEVELOPMENT OF THE COMMUNITY

The European Community began as a formal entity with the signing of the Treaty of Rome in 1957. It was an association of six countries — Belgium, France, Germany, Italy, Luxembourg and the Netherlands — who united to rebuild their countries and achieve lasting peace in Europe, free from the ravages of war. They adopted a *Common Agricultural Policy (CAP)* to ensure the provision of food for their peoples and formed an Iron and Steel Community. **These collaborative enterprises led to greater common understanding and made the confrontations that might have resulted in war between them much less likely.**

One of the major objectives of the Treaty was to remove barriers to trade between the Member States and to create a single integrated internal market. The barriers included monetary controls, customs duties, import and export quotas, immigration controls and restrictions on the formation of companies.

The protracted negotiations to attain the Common Market were further complicated by the accession of six more member states — Denmark, Greece, Ireland, Portugal, Spain and the UK — (the UK joined the Common Market mainly due to the enterprise of two men — Lord Cockfield, the UK's Senior European Commissioner at the time, and Jacques Delors, President of the Commission of the European Community — the Single European Act was signed in 1986 and became effective in 1987.

Negotiations to implement the measures set out in the Act might have continued indefinitely with each member state trying to preserve its own prerogatives. A time limit was set, therefore, that was agreed to be achievable, reasonable and realistic. The date agreed on was 31 December, 1992.

DECISION MAKING IN THE COMMUNITY

The European Council

The Community is run by a *Council of Ministers*. The Council meets five or six times each month. Each of the twelve Member States sends a minister to represent it, the attendance of whom depends on the subjects to be discussed. For example, ministers responsible for economic and financial affairs attend the *'ECO/FIN Council'*. The Foreign Minister is each country's main representative — he or she attends the 'General Affairs Council' which co-ordinates the overall activities of the Council.

In 1974, the Heads of State agreed to meet regularly with the President of the Commission of the European Commission (currently M Jacques Delors) accompanied by their Foreign Ministers. This 'European Council' meets twice a year and is a forum for political co-operation as well as the final approving body for Community legislation.

Many decisions are taken in Council by majority vote. France, Germany, Italy and the UK have 10 votes each; Spain has eight; Belgium, Greece, Netherlands and Portugal have five each; Denmark and Ireland have three each; and Luxembourg has two. A 'qualified majority' decision requires 54 votes out of the possible maximum of 76. There are, however, some issues, particularly those that are related to national sovereignty, such as taxation, where a unanimous decision is required.

The Council is supported by a number of committees and working parties, the most important of which is COREPER, the permanent representative committee consisting of ambassadors to the Community from each Member State. This committee is responsible for preparing proposals from the Commission for presentation to the Council.

The Commission of the European Community

The Commission is a policy planning body whose 17 members are under oath to act independently in the interests of the Community as a whole. Its President is M Jacques Delors. the principle tasks of the Commission are:

—   to make proposals for European laws and policies after consultation with interested parties throughout the Community;

—   to implement Community policies based on Council decisions or on Treaty provisions;

—   to ensure that Community rules and the principles of the European Common Market are respected.

The European Parliament

The Commission is answerable to the 518-member European Parliament which can vote it out of office. The Parliament's members are elected every five years by universal suffrage. France, Germany, Italy and UK each have 81 seats. The Parliament elects a President for each half of the term — Enrique Baron Crespo of Spain was elected President for 1989-1991.

Parliament's role is:

—   consultative and advisory;

— to debate proposed European legislation;

— to propose amendments.

It can influence significantly the details of the Commission's proposals, especially given its increased powers under the Single European Act.

The European Court of Justice

A Court of 13 independent judges settles disputes under Community Law. It has powers to ensure that Community institutions act in accordance with the Treaty and other European legislation. Judgements in the Court also influence the Commission's proposals.

The Council of Europe

There is a *Council of Europe* that should not be confused with the European Council of the Community. The Council of Europe has 23 members including the 12 in the Community, the six in the European Free Trade Association (EFTA), Hungary, Poland, the USSR and Yugoslavia, and is the widest reaching of Europe's political organisations. It provides a valuable forum for collaboration with the Eastern European states.

The Council of Europe deals with a range of issues. One of its successes was the Convention on Human Rights which was signed by all members and ratified by all but one. It also introduced the Convention on Data Protection which has been ratified by nine members including six from the Community. At the end of 1989 it produced a report and guidelines for national legislation on computer-related crime which is dealt with in Chapter 7.

The Process

It takes considerable time for any proposal to be defined by the Commission, debated by the European Parliament, possibly referred back to the Commission for amendment or submitted to

Council for ratification. Thus a topic can become 'news' at each stage and it is essential to understand if it is:

1.   Proposed by the Commission

2.   Accepted by the Parliament, or

3.   Approved by the Council (or by the Commission under delegated authority from the Council).

Only at the third stage does it become Community policy.

It is also important to understand the nature of the legislation. *The Treaty of Rome* is the primary source. Secondary legislation is introduced in order to carry out the basic requirements of the Treaty and can take the form of:

—   *regulations:* these override national laws and are binding on all member states without the need for national legislation;

—   *directives:* these are the most common. They set out requirements for member states to bring their national legislation into conformity with Community policy within a specified period of time;

—   *recommendations:* these are not binding but set out guidelines for national legislation.

THE SINGLE EUROPEAN ACT

The Single European Act set the Community the objective of completing the internal Market and revitalising the common policies before 1 January 1993, in doing so, it provided the Community with the powers it needed to construct a coherent and efficient economic unit (provisions on the internal market, economic and social cohesion, research and monetary policy), while at the same time acknowledging the importance of the quality of life in a community which seeks to be more than just an economic entity (provisions on the environment and social policy). It also reformed the way in which the institutions worked, in order to improve decision-making, give Parliament a bigger say and improve policy-making.

The Commission has completed its programme of 282 proposals dealing with all aspects of the single market — this was achieved two years ahead of the original timetable. Sixty per cent of the programme has already been adopted by the Council, which demonstrates the effectiveness of the new decision-making procedures introduced in the Act. Matters that still require unanimous action by Council are falling behind schedule, however, and member states are still slow to produce national legislation conforming to Community directives, some more so than others; the UK is amongst the leaders in the implementation of the directives.

The dynamic of the internal market is having an effect on intra-Community trade, which after decreasing between 1973 and 1985, has now regained its early 1970s level, accounting for 62 per cent by volume of exports by the member states; this upturn is the most concrete evidence of revitalisation in the economic integration of the Community. At the same time, the Community's place in the world economy has been maintained: between 1985 and 1988 there was a substantial increase in exports.

Industry is planning to step up its level of investment to cope with the increase in demand sparked off by the prospect of 1992. Some firms are taking decisions both on their internal allocation of resources and on external strategies for acquisition and co-operation in preparation for the organisation of the market after 1992. This attitude is founded on the confidence inspired by the pace of work towards the 1992 objective; it is essential that this confidence should not be undermined by the slow progress being made in some areas, especially taxation.

The business environment is giving firms greater freedom within the framework of common rules:

—   In 1992 rules will be introduced on the safety of machinery and will be supplemented by measures on the protection of workers in their place of work.

—   The first stage of liberalising public supply and works contracts became operative during 1990. The opening up of public procurement created opportunities for enterprise and co-operation and led to more rational budgetary expenditure by public authorities. It is estimated that this will lead to savings of ECU 20 billion.

—   In 1992 firms will be able to make their logistics arrangements at Community level.

—   Since 1989 undertakings for collective investment in transferable securities have had access to all markets, placing company bonds and shares in any member country.

—   The freedom of firms to purchase financial services from any bank and to be insured with any company has been largely effected and will be completed by 1992.

—   In 1993 firms will be able to transport goods without restrictions such as quotas, and **carriage of goods internally within a country will be open to any Community company and may not be restricted to that country's carriers.**

—   The establishment of a Europe-wide telecommunications area, by 1992, will enable firms and private citizens to use whatever telecommunications equipment and services they choose provided they are authorised in any member state.

The rights of individuals and businesses are enhanced by legislation, harmonisation and standardisation laid down by Community directives. Since 1989 they have been able to rely on no-fault liability of the manufacturer in the case of accident.

Workers enjoy greater safety at their place of work and greater mobility through the comparability of qualifications. The greatest advance will be made during 1991 with the entry of a general system for the recognition of higher education diplomas; this will open the way to a similar system for other diplomas in 1992, thus allowing mobility in all the professions. *The British Computer Society* has been taking the lead with other professional informatics societies in Europe to establish equivalence of qualifications in informatics.

All students who are able to prove their student status will have the automatic right to receive a residence permit in any Member State.

The main issues covered in the Act are:

1. The Community shall establish an internal market over a period expiring on 31 December 1992 which will ensure the free movement of goods, persons, services and capital. Member states will retain their rights to take measures to combat terrorism, crime, drug trafficking, illicit trading in works of art and antiques, and to control immigration from third world countries. However, to avoid states using these rights to inhibit trade, national controls can be referred to the European Court for adjudication.

2. The Community shall set up a framework for technological research to encourage cooperation between organisations in different member states and provide a firm foundation for industrial innovation. Clearly, the research programmes involving informatics are of considerable interest to suppliers of equipment, and every effort is being made to ensure greater involvement of users. Chapter 4 deals with this topic in detail.

3. For small and medium-sized enterprises (SMEs) the Community will:

    — improve the social, fiscal and administrative environment to promote a spirit of enterprise and healthy competition;

    — encourage co-operation between them; and

— improve access to capital export markets, training and information.

(The definition of an SME used by the Commission is that it must not have more than 500 employees, its net fixed assets must not exceed ECU 75 million and not more than a third of its capital can be held by a larger company. The SPRINT (Strategic Programme for Innovation and Technology Transfer) programme described in Chapter 4 is mainly for the benefit of SMEs in the informatics industrial sector.

4. The Community will continue the policies set out in the Treaty to improve the environment, protect human health and make prudent and rational utilisation of natural resources.

5. Structural funds will be used to reduce the disparities between richer and poorer areas such as rural regions or declining industrial regions. More than ECU 60 billion has been allocated for the period up to 1993 for:

— joint financing of investment and targeted spending in regions where development is lagging;

— regions undergoing conversion;

— combating long-term and youth unemployment;

— improving agricultural, forestry and agri-foodstuffs structures;

— development of rural areas.

6. The European Parliament has been given extended powers to amend legislation through a second reading. If, however, Parliament rejects a proposal on its second reading, it could still be adopted by a unanimous vote in Council.

7. The principle of qualified voting in Council on many issues was accepted and defined (as described above).

IMPLICATIONS OF THE SINGLE MARKET

In order to translate the theoretical principles of the Act into everyday situations, it might be helpful to give a few general examples of its implications:

— Travel: European Community nationals and foreign tourists will no longer be subject to checks at the frontiers between Member State, but will be able to move freely within the Community.

The appropriate government departments are collaborating to deal with terrorism and drug-trafficking. Airlines will operate more flights to a wide variety of destinations (the problems of air traffic control will have been solved!) Fares will be reduced, service will improve and safety will be of the highest standard.

Pending the acceptance of the ECU as a common currency, people will be able to travel throughout the Community with the currency of their choice without restriction. This will have implications for companies' accounting systems in general and 'point-of-sale' systems in particular.

The *Bureau of European Consumer Unions (BEUC)* recently carried out an experiment to see how much it would cost a traveller — in commissions, currency spreads and exchange agencies' profits — just to travel through the Community and change money in each Member State.

Starting out from Brussels with 40,000 Belgian francs, the notional journey went through the Community and back to Brussels. At the end of the trip, 40,000 Belgian francs had turned into 21,300 Belgian francs, a loss of 47 per cent simply from changing the money back and forth into different currencies.

— Students will be able to attend a university in any Member State and study in more than one. Their degrees and diplomas will be recognised throughout the Community.

— Workers, whether employees or self-employed will be able to work in the Member State of their choice, on the same terms as its nationals. Professional qualifications for doctors, lawyers, architects, accountants, etc will be accepted in every Member State regardless of where, in the Community, they were obtained.

— Goods will move freely throughout the Community, without being delayed at the inter-state frontiers since fiscal and administrative constraints, and the associated paperwork, are to be abolished.

— Producers will have access to a genuine market of over 320 million consumers. The harmonisation, or common acceptance, of technical standards, production techniques and composition of products will remove barriers to trade.

— Economies of scale will enable manufacturers to devote more resources to research and technical development, and to offer consumers a wider range of better and cheaper products.

— Health and Safety: Safeguards against dangerous or poisonous products will be raised to the level of the most stringent, as, for example, in the case against the UK over its water supplies. On the other hand, individual Member States cannot insist on mandatory compliance with national safety standards as this would be regarded as a barrier to trade. Thus, some personal computers can be offered for sale in the UK that have not been tested to the standards set by the British Electrotechnical Approval Board (BEAB) or the British Standards Institution (BSI). As long as they meet the Community's Low Voltage Directive, that is sufficient.

— Service companies will be able to offer their services throughout the Community while consumers will be free to choose the best offer in terms of quality and price.

— Road transport will be organised to allow a more rational use of the Community's fleet of trucks (ie lorries will no longer be forced to return home empty). There will be less paperwork, more competition, lower costs and increased safety.

— The range of telecommunications products and services on offer will be highly diversified. It will be based on the latest technologies due to better utilisation of the results of research.

— Financial services organisations, and individuals, will be able to transfer funds freely throughout the Community, and invest wherever they wish. This liberalisation of capital movements will also make it possible to choose the best services available in any member state for mortgages, insurance, leasing, banking, savings, loans, etc even while obtaining the best guarantees.

OTHER COMMUNITY INITIATIVES

Whilst the Single European Act embodies most of the measures needed to achieve the single European market, there are other related initiatives. Moreover, politicians are anxious to point out that trade is not everything — the Community should aim to improve the quality of life for all of its citizens and pursue other moral principles. Some of the initiatives that have implications for companies concerned with informatics, are as follows:

Monetary Union

The European Council at its meeting in June 1989, considered a three stage plan for economic and monetary union (EMU) put forward by the President of the Commission.

The first stage aims to achieve improvement of economic performance, through increasing the co-ordination of economic and monetary policies of the financial institutions in the Member States. It would involve all member states becoming members of the Economic and Monetary System (EMS).

The second stage proposed the establishment of a new institution, the *European System of Central Banks (ESCB)*, which would be independent of national governments and financial institutions. The ESCB would aim to reduce the variations in exchange rates.

The third stage proposes full economic and monetary union. The Heads of States, with the exception of the then Prime Minister of the UK, welcomed the plan. The UK objected on the grounds that stage two would require changes to the Community's Treaties, too soon after the passing of the Single European Act in July 1987, and that stage three would require political union as the Council would be able to determine national budgets.

Finance Ministers of the Member States agreed the initial preparations for Stage One at a meeting in July 1989, and set up an Inter-Governmental Conference (IGC) to consider changes to the EC Treaties.

Pierre Beregovoy, the French Finance Minister, and Henning Christopherson, the commissioner responsible for economic and monetary affairs, stressed the importance of the timetable for the implementation of the decisions reached on economic and monetary union. Christopherson pointed out that member states will have a reasonable period of adaptation before the coming into force of Phase One of EMU.

Community Company Statute

In July 1989, the Commission tabled a modified plan for a Company Statute which will permit a European Company to be formed by companies from two or more member states by mergers or joint subsidiaries, free from the company laws of the member states in which they do business. The part of the legislation that has caused most difficulty concerns worker participation. Martin Bangemann (the commissioner responsible for the internal market) said that "there will be no European Company without a clear definition of the way in which workers participate in the decisions". Three models were set out for worker participation: one based on the German co-determination scheme in which workers elect between one-third to a half of the members of a supervisory board; a system of workers' consultative committees; and a loose arrangement under which collective bargaining agreements make some general provision for workers to be given information about company plans that will affect them.

Cross-border Mergers

After years of tough and complex negotiations, Ministers of the Community's countries have agreed regulations for vetting large cross-border mergers. The new system may involve around 40 multi-million pound takeovers being subject to the approval of the Commission each year. Under the scheme, which commenced operation for four years from 21 September, 1990, the Commission will have the sole authority to investigate and — where it deems fit — veto mergers involving trans-national companies with a combined turnover of more than ECU 5.5 billion per annum. This will apply where at least two of the firms earn ECU 250 million or more of that turnover in the Community but do not earn more than two thirds of their total turnover in a single Member State. In addition, proposed mergers involving companies with a turnover of less than ECU 2 billion, may be examined by the Commission at the request of an effected Member State. All other mergers will fall under the jurisdiction of national authorities where such authorities exist.

Social Charter

The Commission has outlined the elements that could be included in a *Charter of Fundamental Social Rights*. They are:

— the right to work;

— rights regarding working conditions;

— the right to have a written contract of employment;

— the right to social services, including a minimum level of income;

— the right to education, professional or vocational training and further education;

— the right to form associations, including collective bargaining and the right to (or not to) strike;

— the right to work anywhere in the Community (this implies common acceptance of qualifications);

— equality of sexes with regard to pay, opportunities in employment and social benefits;

— workers' rights to have information about, consultation on and participation in the management of their companies;

— protection of the elderly and the right to flexible retirement.

The European Parliament supports this Charter. It had prepared its own *Declaration of Fundamental Rights and Liberties* that had the same objectives. Chancellor Kohl of Germany, who supports the Charter, is quoted as saying "In creating the Single Market, we cannot ignore the 80 per cent who are workers." The Prime Minister of the UK was the only member of the Council to oppose the Charter on the grounds that it would interfere with national, social policy-making and would impose a burden that would make the Community less competitive in international markets.

EXTERNAL RELATIONSHIPS

EFTA

There are six countries in the *European Free Trade Association (EFTA)* — Austria, Finland, Iceland, Norway, Sweden and Switzerland. Regular talks have been in progress between the Community and EFTA since 1984. The aim being to create a 19-nation (including Lichtenstein) *European Economic Space*, probably by 1993, in which virtually all barriers to the free movement of goods, services, capital and people will be removed. However, the Community will not compromise its autonomy and the supremacy of its political institutions; the European Parliament in particular. There are also reservations within EFTA:

none of its members accepts the *Common Agricultural Policy* and some are reluctant to allow the free movement of people from the Community. EFTA has more stringent environmental standards than the Community which could inhibit free trade in, for example, cars. Some individual members of EFTA have particular objections, for example, Iceland on fishing rights and Switzerland on financial services. Others are negotiating separately to join the Community. Austria has already made a formal application.

Nevertheless, the European Economic Space may provide one of the most important means of forming a new economic and political order in Europe, possibly with the eventual inclusion of Eastern European countries.

EFTA collaborates with the Community on a number of research and development projects as part of a general high technology programme known as EUREKA. Turkey is also a member of EUREKA. The total number of projects launched since EUREKA's creation in 1985 is 385 with a total budget of ECU 7.8 billion. Eighteen organisations in the UK participate in 95 of the projects.

USSR and Eastern Europe

In December 1989, a ten year trade and co-operation agreement was signed between the Community and the Soviet Union. The Soviet Foreign Minister, Eduard Shevardnadze, described the agreement as a major economic building block in the foundation of a 'common European home', and called for the initiative to be pushed forward by the establishment of a tripartite commission of the Community, EFTA and COMECON (see Glossary). The agreement opens the way for collaboration on issues ranging from nuclear safety to technology transfer. Roland Dumas, French Foreign Minister and President of the Council at that time, said the agreement allowed for the development of even closer relations and would open the way to a "political dialogue on the many matters of common interest to all in Europe."

The rapid change towards democracy in Eastern states is acting as a catalyst to accelerate progress to economic and monetary union in the Community, as many Europeans regard this as the best way to provide a political and economic focus for those states.

Investment in informatics has been low in Eastern Europe, partly due to the economic priorities (food and housing are more essential than computers) and partly due to the prohibition of high technology exports by *COCOM* (the Co-ordinating Committee for Multilateral Export Controls). The member countries of Cocom are the 16 nations in the North Atlantic Treaty Organisation and Japan. The USA has been the main opponent of high technology exports to Eastern Europe on the grounds that they might be used to improve military strength. In June 1990, however, the President of the USA, Mr George Bush, proposed that some 30 categories of goods and technologies (including a number of personal and mainframe computers, peripherals and storage devices, and a variety of telecommunications equipment) be removed from the list of 120 restricted items and that regulations on exporting 13 other items should be relaxed.

This is important for the informatics industries in the Community since the low level of provision in Eastern Europe makes it a fertile market-place. No doubt this was one of the reasons for the USA's change in attitude as it may be expected that American companies are well-placed to exploit this market.

USA

There are two conflicting views of the Community taken by American companies. The more positive view is that the removal of barriers will improve the opportunities for companies to market and sell their products throughout the Community.

Many American suppliers of informatics equipment, such as Amdahl, Apple, Digital and IBM, have set up pan-European sales, marketing and service organisations. They have, indeed, looked upon Europe as a unified market to a much geater extent than European companies who are more concerned with national differences.

Some American suppliers have also set up manufacturing plants in Europe. Digital, for example, has plants in Ireland, France, Germany and the Netherlands as well as the UK, and Amdahl has a plant in Ireland.

The negative apprehension expressed by some American companies is that the Community will become a trading 'fortress', setting up protectionist measures to give preferment to its own industry. This is partly a reflection of policies that have been introduced in the USA to protect the internal market there. Many Americans see the threat of a more united European industry compounding the threat from Japan to their internal industry.

In fact, the requirements of users of informatics equipment and services will ensure that they seek the most appropriate and cost-effective solution available in the market, regardless of the country or origin. Since many of these solutions are obtainable from the USA, there is no possibility of excluding American companies from the European market.

In recent years, the informatics market in Europe has grown faster than the market in the USA and this is likely to continue for several more years, particularly as Eastern European countries start to catch up with the applications of informatics. Thus, there will be ample scope for both American and European companies to expand to meet the increasing demand.

Japan

Japanese suppliers of informatics systems have been quick to realise the opportunities offered by the single European market. Their approach has been to buy their way into the Community by taking shares in European companies. At the time of writing, Fujitsu is making a bid for a controlling share in ICL. Mitsubishi has taken control of Apricot, and Oki Europe, a subsidiary of the Japanese electronics company Oki Electronic, is planning to acquire the data business of Technitron, one of its main distributors of printers in the UK. Further examples can be found in the pages of the newspapers and computer press each week.

One aspect of Japanese trade that has been causing concern is the practice of 'dumping'. Some Japanese companies have been selling equipment at greatly reduced prices in an effort to swamp the market and, presumably, put European competitors out of business. The Commission has introduced levies to inhibit this practice. There were 27 such cases between 1980 and 1989 representing only 2 per cent of total Japanese exports to the Community in that period. Nevertheless, the Commission has had to defend its actions at meetings of the GATT countries where Japan has lodged complaints.

On the other hand, the Commission has persuaded Member States to give up their nationally imposed quotas on Japanese goods, and these restrictions have dropped sharply from 130 at the end of 1988 to 56 by the end of 1989.

Over recent years, there has been a rapid growth in economic activity between the Community and Japan. The value of trade, for example, increased from ECU 19 billion in 1980 to over ECU 67 billion in 1989. The Community absorbs some 18 per cent of Japanese exports and 19 per cent of Japanese foreign investment. In 1989, there were 411 Japanese owned manufacturing companies in the Community, each employing an average of some 350 Europeans. Community exports to Japan have been increasing at a rate of 20 per cent each year since 1987.

The Commission is committed to redressing the imbalance of trade with Japan in accordance with internationally agreed principles laid down by GATT, and has set up a joint committee with Japan to accelerate the correction of this imbalance.

The imbalance in trade is matched by an imbalance in direct investment. The cumulative total of Japanese investment in the Community to March 1989 was about ECU 23 billion, 14 times greater than the Community's cumulative investment in Japan. The Commission has, therefore, paid for a study of investment opportunities in Japan for European companies which will be published during 1990.

DIRECTORATE GENERAL XIII

The Commission is divided into a number of Directorates General. That of greatest relevance to informatics is Directorate General (DG) XIII under M Michel Carpentier which is concerned with telecommunications, information industries and innovation. The commissioner responsible for DGXIII and its areas of interest is Sr Filippo Mario Pandolfi. DG XIII is responsible for many research and development programmes (described in Chapter 4). The main one is the *European Strategic Programme for Research and Development in Information Technology (ESPRIT)*.

DG XIII is also responsible for telecommunications policy and a number of applications programmes in such areas as education and training, transport, health care and administrative informatics.

The address is:

DIRECTORATE GENERAL XIII
Commission of the European Communities
Breydel Building
Avenue d'Auderghem, 45
1040-Brussels
Belgium

Telephone: 010 322 235 1111 or +322 235 1111

2 The Informatics Industry

INTRODUCTION

This chapter details the progress in recent years of European companies that supply informatics systems, suggests reasons for the improvement and the need to sustain effort.

IMPROVEMENT OF THE EUROPEAN INFORMATICS INDUSTRY

At the beginning of the 1980s, the European informatics industry was descending down a vicious spiral. Low market share led to low investment in research and development (R&D) and capital investment. The lack of investment made it difficult to keep up with the new and improved products being developed by American and Japanese companies. The failure to produce competitive products resulted in a lower share of the market. And so on down the spiral.

Since 1984, there have been some encouraging trends with European suppliers of computing systems, in total, almost doubling their revenues. Table 2.1, derived from Datamation figures, shows that, in 1988, they held six of the top ten places in the list of suppliers of systems in Europe.

Moreover, five European companies are in the top ten when the growth rate, (of the top twenty IT companies is examined) measured in terms of percentage increase in revenue (see Table 2.2).

Rank	Firm	Country	Information System in Europe ($ M)	Total IS Sales Worldwide ($ M)
1	IBM	US	20,500	55,000
2	Siemens	Germany	5,300	5,900
3	DEC	US	4,400	12,300
4	Olivetti	Italy	4,400	5,400
5	Bull	France	4,000	5,300
6	Nixdorf	Germany	2,800	3,000
7	Unisys	US	2,600	9,100
8	Hewlett-Packard	US	2,300	6,300
9	Philips	Netherlands	2,200	2,800
10	STC (ICL)	UK	2,100	2,400
	TOTAL		90,000	

Table 2.1: IT System Suppliers in Europe, 1988

			Preliminary estimate (%)
Bull			40
		Toshiba	22
Olivetti			19
Nixdorf	Apple	NEC	16
	DEC		15
		Hitachi	14
Siemens			13
ICL	NCR		12
	HP		11
	Xerox	Fujitsu	10
	IBM		6
	Wang		6
Philips	Unisys		3
	CDC		3

Table 2.2: Top IT Companies ranked by 1984-1987 Average Yearly Revenue Increase in National Currency

There has also been a rising trend in European cross-frontier mergers, amalgamations and collaboration in which a number of the major European informatics companies have been involved. In 1983, the number of European alliances was small, particularly compared with the alliances being formed with non-European organisations. European companies were more likely to look towards the US for strategic alliances, but, as shown in Figure 2.1, the situation has changed considerably. The number of European alliances increased by a factor of seven over four years, and this does not include the strategically important links that have been formed on the pre-competitive R&D projects, such as the ESPRIT programme. Rather, the situation reported in the figure refers to concrete company agreements on joint ventures and mergers, way beyond any agreements on just R&D projects. Obviously, European industry is now capitalising on European-wide technological co-operation, and a restructuring of the industry machinery is now happening as a prelude to the opening-up of the European market in 1992.

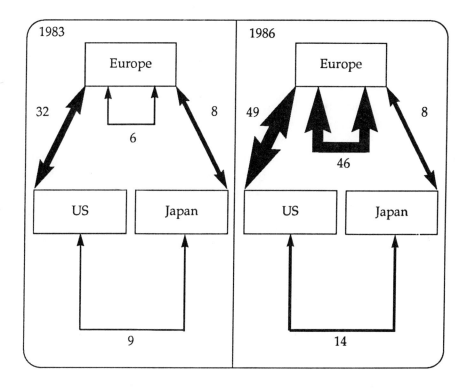

Figure 2.1: Cross Border Alliances between IT Companies

REASONS FOR PROGRESS

There are many reasons for the improvement in the performance of these European companies.

— The technological base has been strengthened by Community programmes, such as ESPRIT, and national R&D programmes, such as ALVEY in the UK.

— There has been increased collaboration between organisations in different member states and between industry and academic institutions — also brought about by these programmes.

— Changes in management practices have also made a significant contribution. Many companies have been through a tough internal rationalisation process.

— Cross-frontier mergers and amalgamations have resulted in larger companies with consequent economies of scale in research, development, marketing and sales.

— Companies have reduced their margins and compressed their profits in order to invest in R&D and capital expenditure. They have done this even whilst coping with the deterioration in the balance of trade in those components of informatics systems which have had to be imported, particularly integrated circuits and peripherals. In the second half of the 1980s, the combined R&D and capital investments of major European companies grew faster than those of major US and Japanese competitors and are now at the level of 18 per cent of their turnover, the same as that of US companies.

THE NEED TO SUSTAIN EFFORT

To secure a competitive industry, a high level of R&D spending will have to be maintained or even increased. The Community will have to continue its catalytic role through collaborative programmes. More specific action is required, however, to ensure that all this R&D effort is not wasted. There must be a programme of 'technology transfer' to ensure that results are properly disseminated and taken up by innovators, manufacturers, service providers and the end users.

The many initiatives taken by companies to restructure and rationalise must continue until they form units that will be viable in global terms. In this process it is inevitable that some companies will go out of business but those remaining will be better able to compete in world markets. It is better to have a few strong companies than many weak ones that are bound to perish in the long-term and, in the meantime, drain away resources that could be used to improve the competitiveness of other firms.

Major European informatics users still too often have to purchase systems from America or Japan, because the demands of competition do not allow them to wait for European suppliers to catch up. Europe's informatics suppliers must continue to improve their position amongst the systems that are needed within the Community. There will need to be greater collaboration between users and suppliers, possibly through ESPRIT, in order to develop these systems. Forty per cent of ESPRIT projects have involved the participation of at least one user company, and this has contributed know-how essential for success in marketing products derived from project results.

SEMICONDUCTORS

The situation in semiconductors is not encouraging. Foreign firms dominate this most important sector of the market. Japan supplies about 50 per cent of the semiconductors in Europe, with US firms supplying about 40 per cent and European firms about 11 per cent. In the top ten league table only Philips figures for Europe, at seventh place. Japanese firms occupy the top three places (see Table 2.3). The market is dominated by the 'standard' suppliers of memory and microprocessor chips. For some years, Philips and Siemens have worked together on the Megachip project. They were joined in the JESSI (Joint European Submicron Silicon Initiative) project by Thomson and Cap-Gemini-Sogetti (CGS) together with other firms like Inmos and Plessey. Their governments are supporting the project through the EUREKA scheme; the Community will be involved through the next stage of ESPRIT. The objective of the JESSI project is to put 64 million bits on a chip which is intended to reach the market in about 1997. This is intended to enable Europe to play a significant part in the world semiconductor industry.

Rank	Firm	Country	$bn
1	NEC	Japan	3.2
2	Toshiba	Japan	3.0
3	Hitachi	Japan	2.8
4	Motorola	USA	2.4
5	Texas Instruments	USA	2.1
6	Fujitsu	Japan	1.9
7	Philips	Netherlands	1.6
8	Intel	USA	1.5
9	Mitsubishi	Japan	1.5
10	Matsushita	Japan	1.5
	Overall Sales		36.6

Table 2.3: Top Ten Semiconductor Suppliers

Rank	Firm	Country	1987 $Bn
1	MEI/JVC	Japan	100
2	Sony	Japan	62
3	Philips	Europe	50
4	Thomson/GE/RCA	Europe	45
5	Hitachi	Japan	37
6	Toshiba	Japan	37
7	Mitsubishi	Japan	25
8	Sanyo	Japan	24
9	Samsung	Korea	23
10	Goldstar	Korea	20

Table 2.4: Consumer Electronics (Audio and Video)

In consumer electronics, two European firms are in the top ten (Table 2.4), which is totally dominated by Japanese and, now, Korean firms. In this field, and that of computer peripherals, the balance of trade is bad.

SOFTWARE

In the software field, American firms have a significant part of the market through the software that comes with their computers and through standard packages for personal computers. The European bespoke industry has an excellent reputation in the world and dominates this part of the European market, but it has not succeeded in taking as large a share of the market outside Europe as its excellence might lead one to expect. This is probably due to the fragmented nature of the market in Europe, and the usual problem in the European industry of failure to invest enough in marketing overseas. The French have been steadily consolidating their industry, and CGS is the largest software house in Europe. In this section of the industry much consolidation is necessary, and is beginning to happen.

TELECOMMUNICATIONS

The convergence of telecommunications and computer technology is transforming the industrial and socio-economic fabric of Europe as a result of spectacular developments in three areas in particular:

— Microelectronics ('chips');

— Digitisation of telecommunications (application of 'computer language' to functions such as switching and transmission);

— New transmission technologies (optical fibres, satellites).

Worldwide, the market created by these developments already exceeds ECU 500 billion. By the year 2000, up to 7 per cent of the Community's GDP may derive from telecommunications, compared with just over 2 per cent currently. By the end of the century, up to 60 per cent of all jobs will be dependent to a greater or lesser extent on telecommunications through information technology integration.

Total exports of telecommunications equipment from the Community rose by 22 per cent in nominal terms between 1988 and 1989 and imports rose by 23 per cent. The Community market for telecommunications equipment is estimated at ECU 23.1 billion in 1988 and ECU 24.7 billion in 1989. This means that Community trade as a proportion of market size rose from about 16 per cent to over 18 per cent between 1988 and 1989.

The future competitiveness and prosperity of the European telecommunications industry calls for action on two main fronts: the scale of the market, and its future organisation. No single Community country accounts for more than 6 per cent of the world's telecommunications market, whereas the United States represents 35 per cent and Japan 11 per cent. Yet, taken as a whole, the Community has a 20 per cent world market share. The potential of the single market offers great opportunities for the European industry, and it is evident that the Community needs more competitive market structures.

The regulations for the future markets in telecommunications equipment and services are being redefined. The Commission's Green Paper, issued in 1987, attempted to ensure that this redefinition takes place in a rapid, orderly and effective way, to make the most use of the new economic opportunities offered by advanced telecommunications throughout the Community. The basic idea and aim of the Green Paper was the establishment of a competitive Community-wide telecommunications market by 1992.

The Green Paper was widely welcomed, and the positive response has been followed up by a series of actions, including a strict time schedule with the following main points:

—   The complete opening of terminal equipment markets by 31 December 1990;

—   Progressive opening of the market for telecommunications services from 1989 onwards;

— Full mutual recognition of type approvals;

— Full opening of the receiving antenna market before 31 December 1989, except where they are connected to public networks;

— The setting up of a European Telecommunications Standards Institute (ETSI), as described in Chapter 6, following agreement with the European Conference of Postal Telecommunications Administrations (CEPT).

Actions are also being pursued on:

— Progressive implementation of post-oriented telecommunications tariffs;

— Application of VAT to telecommunications;

— Full application of Community competition rules to the sector;

— Ensuring independence of procurement of telecommunications administrations and the opening of public procurement.

Discussions are still continuing on:

— A coherent European position regarding the future regulation and development of satellite communications in the Community;

— A concept for the promotion of Europe-wide services, by a market-led approach and definition of common tariff principles;

— Defining a European position on the major international questions in telecommunications;

— Developing the social dialogue and taking full account of social concerns.

To support the proposals within the Green Paper the collaborative RACE (Research and Development in

Advanced Communication technologies in Europe) programme
was launched to develop the Integrated Broadband
Communications Network (see Chapter 4). From a political point
of view, the RACE programme has had to acknowledge the roles
of the PTTs (National authorities for postal, telephone and
telecommunications services) within the Community. Within the
Member States, the role of the PTTs varies widely, some
preferring totally public operation, others looking for full
privatisation. The RACE programme provides the framework in
which the technical problems can be solved, whilst providing the
vehicle for industrial integration and political consensus on future
telecommunications services.

THE SKILLS SHORTAGE

One of the factors that is likely to inhibit growth of the informatics
industries is the shortage of qualified people, particularly those
skilled in software development and applications. It is estimated
that there are about two million computer professionals in
Europe. The graduate part of this body is growing at about 8 per
cent per annum although the percentage varies from country to
country. It is going to be difficult to sustain this growth since the
demographic trends in most of the European countries shows a
steady decline in the numbers coming onto the job market (see
Figure 2.2). The UK is reasonably typical: over a 12-year period
from the peak in 1983 to the trough in 1995 there will be a fall of
about 30 per cent in the 18-year olds coming onto the job market.
In Germany the fall is steeper and somewhat deeper. In France
the situation is not quite so bad; in Italy the fall was delayed for
a few years, but then was as steep as elsewhere in Europe.
Indeed, only Ireland shows an upward trend in 18-year olds.

The continued expansion of the informatics market will be
driven in the next decade largely by improved cost effectiveness
in communications, due to fibre optics and digital cellular radio,
and by the growth of new applications stemming from artificial
intelligence work. It is clear that this expansion will not continue
if there is a shortage of skilled manpower.

A possible remedy for this situation is to improve the efficiency
of software production which is a labour-intensive activity.

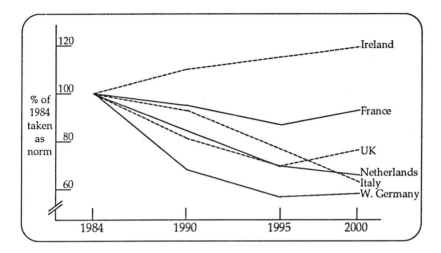

Figure 2.2: 15-19 Year olds in Western Europe

Productivity can be considerably improved by widespread application of software productivity methods and tools that already exist and are being applied by leading firms. This remedy is being pursued by the Community through the European Systems and Software Initiative (ESSI). This programme is a major drive to improve the productivity of software production across Europe by applying methods and tools through an awareness programme to draw attention to these methods, and, perhaps most important of all, through a drive on training, especially of the trainers.

More can be done to widen the catchment area for people entering the industry. In much of Europe the percentage of women in the profession is low and there is a great deal of scope for improving the opportunities for women. More, too, can be done by widening the scope for mixed degrees containing informatics as a major subject, combined with business studies, languages or, indeed, almost any other subject. Experience has shown that people with such joint degrees are particularly valuable in the applications of informatics. In the UK, the growth of degrees involving languages with informatics is also helping to remedy the traditional weakness in languages.

THE ELEMENTS FOR SUCCESS

The European informatics industry will only fully succeed in meeting the challenge of the single market if, in parallel with internal market unification, it can systematically strengthen the research and development effort; define the appropriate regulations to control the market; and develop a united approach to competing in world markets.

There needs to be greater confidence in the future for both the business community and consumers. This requires common standards and convergent strategies guiding the decisions of commercial companies, public and private service suppliers, and consumer demand. For example, the definition of co-ordinated strategies in the Community for progress towards Integrated Services Digital Network (ISDN) and second-generation mobile telephony will harmonise conditions for the supply of the corresponding products and services, and will stimulate demand.

Users need to get involved in order to influence the informatics industry as regards product definition, adaptation of sales strategies, etc so that the industry can benefit from a strong, resounding and diversified demand on a continental scale. Strong demand means that considerable improvements must be made to the conditions of access to new products and services for professional and domestic users, mainly through:

— The adoption of common standards, guaranteeing compatibility and interoperability;

— The establishment of basic infrastructure allowing the new informatics and audiovisual products, services and equipment to be fully utilised within an integrated framework — hence the importance attached to the progress made in co-ordinated strategies for telecommunications;

— Harmonisation of conditions of access to telecommunications networks, in particular, charging principles, vital to the achievement of a unified informatics services market, which will encourage users to acquire and use the new equipment and services.

Demand in Europe will be receptive to innovation and the supply of new products and services only if certain psychological and cultural barriers can be overcome. A special effort is required to make the new technologies part of our working and leisure lives, constantly bearing in mind the need to seek maximum user-friendliness of interfaces, so as to develop efficient tools suited to a wide variety of requirements.

3 Industrial Competitiveness and Strategies

INTRODUCTION

One of the main points that has been made in the preceding chapters is that US and Japanese companies are often better placed to exploit the advantages of trading within a unified European market than the European companies. This is due, in part, to the fragmented nature of the European informatics industry, with many relatively small firms concentrating mainly on markets within their own country. In contrast, many large US companies already conduct some elements of their business on a truly European scale and are well advanced in preparing strategies for 1992; some Japanese companies are buying shares in European companies to pave their way into Europe — the takeover of ICL by Fujitsu is a typical example.

The Community has allocated considerable resources to research and technological development in an effort to increase collaboration across national boundaries, and also between industry and educational institutions. The intention is that by developing working relationships, mutual respect and trust when collaborating in non-competitive areas, companies will be encouraged to collaborate in developing products or services, manufacturing and marketing.

The Community has also set up, or helped to set up, bodies to help industry carry the results of R&D through to marketable products and services. Since these could help to improve competitiveness, details of three initiatives (SPRINT, TII and BC-NET) are described at the end of this chapter. Particular attention is being paid to small and medium enterprises (SMEs) as they are least likely to be able to compete with large companies in international markets. However, European organisations cannot rely solely on Community initiatives — even assuming that they are willing to participate in collaborative projects and programmes. They will need to take account of the European dimension in formulating their business plans and strategies.

This chapter indicates some of the activities that need to be addressed. Many organisations will be aware of some of these issues already. There is no harm done by reiterating the need for action — the great danger is that by omitting to pursue these actions European organisations will yield up the opportunities of the single market to others outside the Community.

Many of the suggestions will be of interest to all organisations, academic and research institutions as well as industrial and commercial companies. Indeed, there is plenty of advice available from other sources. In the UK the Department of Trade and Industry provides a great deal of helpful literature which can be obtained by telephoning 081 200 1992. Some issues are more relevant to suppliers of informatics equipment and services. Others relate to users of informatics and are concerned with the effect of Community activities and legislation on their IT or DP systems. The main thrust, however, is to encourage organisations to revise their business strategies so that informatics is used to the greatest extent possible to contribute to their competitiveness.

As a skeleton for the first part of this chapter, I have drawn from the booklet by John Drew, Head of the UK Offices of the Commission, *Europe 1992 — Developing an Active Company Approach to the European Market*. The strategy he proposes a 'European Audit', is based on activities already carried out by several companies in preparation for 1992.

I have also included a section on the scope for developing a marketing strategy throughout the Community, since many companies are still relying on their national customers and are not exploiting the possible benefits of the larger sales base offered by the single European market.

By extending their customer base, companies should be aware of the improved communication, made possible by using electronic data interchange (EDI). A further section describes EDI — what it is and how it can contribute to competitiveness.

DEVELOPING A EUROPEAN STRATEGY

The following steps should be considered as a means of raising the awareness of an organisation to the implications of the single European market and increasing its competitiveness in global markets by exploiting its position within the Community.

Step 1 — Inform and Involve Top Management

The first step is to obtain commitment from top management by highlighting the need to take account of the single European market in future business plans and strategies. Commitment stems from conviction. Senior managers must be convinced that there is a serious risk of competition from other countries taking away the organisation's business if they do not take a positive attitude to the opportunities and challenges.

It is recommended that a short seminar should be arranged for senior managers and members of the board to discuss the following issues:

— The need to identify competitors from other countries, in Europe and elsewhere, who may take advantage of the single market to sell products or services at lower prices or higher quality to the organisation's customers. The effect that this is likely to have on profitability should be estimated.

— The scope for increasing sales volumes in other Community countries. The effect that the increased sales might have on pricing structures and profitability. The savings in the cost of trading throughout the Community as a result of barriers being removed. A figure of ECU 200 billion is often quoted as the financial burden that is borne by citizens and companies in the Community due to the internal barriers to trade. This implies that a potential saving of this magnitude can be achieved when the single market has been established. The benefits will be most apparent in lower prices and lower costs but there will also be benefits from social and political change. The research that led to this conclusion is set out in an easy-to-read book *The European Challenge — 1992, the benefits of a single market* by Paolo Cecchini.

— New ways of doing business. In particular, the use of electronic data interchange (EDI) to improve external communications with customers and suppliers.

— Collaboration in Community programmes on R&D, or education and training. The European Strategic Programme for Research and Development in Information Technology (ESPRIT), described in Chapter 4, applies to anyone working in informatics, whether as user, supplier or researcher. The basic rules are that at least two organisations from different countries in the EC must be involved and one, at least, must be an industrial or commercial company. The industrial partner is expected to meet half of its own costs. There are also programmes with other industrial sectors that have a significant informatics content — DRIVE in transport and AIM in health services, for example.

— Collaboration with other companies which may have complementary skills in product development, manu-facture, sales or marketing. In marketing particularly, there is likely to be increasing collaboration between organisations in different Member States. It may be possible to use an organisation in another member state to act as a marketing agent or, conversely, to do the marketing for another European organisation in the home country. The SPRINT programme, described below, can help to identify possible partners.

— The effect on the informatics system of changes in European legislation on:

   • technical standards;

   • currency;

- taxation;

- company accounts;

- data protection;

- security against unauthorised access;

- software copyright.

— The cost of pursuing the new strategy, including the cost of employing consultants in areas where the organisation has no expertise.

It is advisable to provide briefing material prior to the meeting such as John Drew's booklet *Europe 1992 — Developing an Active Company Approach to the European Market* mentioned earlier. It should be emphasised that the meeting is a prelude to, not a substitution for, action. In order to sustain the action, it is advisable that a senior manager, preferably at board level, should be responsible for adding a European dimension to the business plan. This 'European Director' should be provided with up-to-date information such as the newsletter *IT in Europe* available from A Plus Publications (Telephone 0753 586655 or + 44 753 586655) or, for information on collaborative projects, the publication *Interface Europe* (Telephone 0235 811 536 or + 44 235 811536). This director may also assess the effects on the organisation of the various directives and regulations coming out of the Community.

The Commission maintains an up-to-date online database of regulations, directives and decisions plus proposals under consideration and judgements of the European Court of Justice. This is known as *Celex*, and information about access and charges can be obtained from:

Eurobase
Commission of the European Communities
Rue de la Loi, 200
1049-BRUSSELS
Belgium

Telephone: 010 322 235 0001/3 or + 322 235 0001/3

In the UK, the Department of Trade and Industry maintains a similar database called *Spearhead,* this lists the measures relevant to the creation of the single market (For details telephone 081 200 1992 or + 44 81 200 1992).

Step 2 — Inform and Involve the Rest of the Organisation

The information, comment and debate should then be transmitted down through the organisation to managers and supervisors until the entire organisation is committed to facing the challenge of the single market. This will require seminars and discussions to increase the level of awareness and concern with the issues.

Step 3 — Conduct a European Audit

John Drew suggests that each organisation should consider conducting a European audit — "strengths and weaknesses" approach to the prospects of the organisation in relation to the single market. It is by no means the only way to go about forming a strategy, but it is a method that has proved successful in many companies.

The steps in such an audit are as follows:

— Obtain the Commission's 1985 White Paper and supporting documents, such as progress reports and sectorial analyses.

— Identify the proposals which seem relevant to the organisation. (For the informatics industry standardisation proposals, among others, would be especially relevant). Some will have obvious costs or benefits in bottom-line terms; it will be more difficult to put a price tag on others. They might, however, be even more important as signposts to further essential preparatory activity.

— List the organisation's departments, or areas of activity, and apportion the proposals among them.

— Write a short four or five line description of each proposal and an initial assessment of how it might affect the department. Send these with a covering letter and a short background note to every head of department.

— Set up a meeting with the heads of departments and other staff to discuss the information sent to them. These are key meetings, as each manager will need to be convinced of the importance and relevance of the measures for his function.

— Refine the proposals and take up detailed points with trade associations, chambers of commerce, consultants, relevant government departments or offices/directorates of the Commission. Lobbying in the Commission or Parliament for the organisation's priorities and goals should be considered, as decisions made there, may well have significant effect on the organisation's viability. European Paliament contacts can be made through local MEPs as well as with the Parliament itself:

> European Parliament
> Palais de l'Europe
> 67070-STRASBOURG
> France.
>
> Telephone: 010 33 88 17 4001 or + 33 88 17 4001

— Refer back to company departments. Assess costs benefits, implications and necessary actions of each proposal. Track how far each proposal has got in the European legislative process and its likely date of implementation.

— Update senior management on progress so far and agree further steps.

At this stage a decision may be made to abandon activity as having achieved its first objective of making senior management aware of the implications of the single market.

Alternatively, it may be considered desirable to pursue the issues further. In which case it may be useful to draw up a base document to track progress which explains the following:

— the decision making process of the Community;

— the key proposals and implications for specific departments;

— implications for the organisation as a whole;

— how the audit can be integrated into the organisation's
  strategy development.

A system will need to be set up for regular update and review
of material. The actual research and work to be done will vary
greatly among organisations, even companies in the same
industry. Smaller organisations, which may not have the
necessary management resources should consider buying in
consultancy to support their effort, or simply using channels
other than their own to develop a single market strategy. Some
channels that can be used are trade associations or commercial
and public seminars. In the UK, the Department of Trade and
Industry will usually prove initial consultancy under its *Enterprise
Initiative* free of charge, and make a contribution to the cost of any
further consultancy that may be recommended as being
necessary. Details are available from local DTI offices or by
telephoning 0800 500 200.

Formulation of plans and auditing an organisation's strengths
and weaknesses will undoubtedly require contacts with national
and   Community   institutions.   The   Commission's
DirectoratesGeneral III, IV, XIII, XV and XXI deal respectively
with questions of the internal market and industrial affairs;
competition policy; telecommunications, information industries
and innovation, financial institutions and company law, and
customs union and indirect taxation.

They can all be contacted through:

The Commission of the European Communities
Rue de la Loi, 200
1040-BRUSSELS
Belgium.

Telephone: 010 322 235 1111 or + 322 235 1111.

Companies concerned with informatics will want to keep in contact with DG XIII as well as standards institutions such as *The British Standards Institute (BSI)* in the UK, the *European Committee for Standardisation (CEN)*, the *European Committee for Electrotechnical Standardisation (CENELEC)* and the *Conference of European Postal and Telecommunications Administrations (CEPT)*, (addresses are given in Chapter 6).

MARKETING

Some Member States are lagging in the use of informatics and are anxious to catch up with the rest of the Community. These countries, therefore, offer great potential for sales of hardware, software and services. The attractions of these markets are:

— There is rapid growth in applications — with consequent opportunities for large sales volumes.

— They can use the latest technology uninhibited by investment in, or the need for compatibility with, old technology.

— There is little competition from the indigenous industry — although, of course, other companies from the Community and elsewhere will also try to realise the same marketing opportunities.

One way of establishing a foothold in these countries is to establish a base there. Apart from the potential for large sales, there are additional advantages arising from low labour, property and other operating costs. Moreover, development funds are available both from the local government that wishes to build up its own informatics industry and from the Community's Regional Development Fund.

Against this there are difficulties to be overcome. Language is an obvious one. Cultural differences, which may vary from region to region within the same country, exist particularly in the ways of conducting business. Contract law in most of Europe is based on the Napoleonic code which is less structured and relies less on precedent than the UK system. Payment can take a long time, sometimes many months, particularly when dealing with the public sector. And, as is usual in all marketing, it is important to build up personal contacts, particularly with politicians and public officials when seeking public sector orders.

Measures that impact on market opportunities include the proposals to reduce frontier controls on the movements of goods within the Community and the moves to simplify and harmonise internal trade procedures. A major turning point was the standardisation of data requirements brought about by the introduction of the Single Administrative Document (SAD), which replaced about a hundred forms used in trade between Member States, and a common integrated tariff. For the foreseeable future, systems will continue to be needed to deal with fiscal requirements, notably with the differences in VAT between Member States. There will also be a continuing requirement to collect, in some form, statistics on intra-Community trade (which have been derived from the SAD since January 1988). At present, both are dealt with at the various frontiers, but in future they could, for example, be handled on the basis of cross-border transport. There is, therefore, considerable scope for the introduction of informatics systems. One can see the possibilty of their integration with the rapidly growing systems for electronic data interchange (EDI) between importers and exporters, port and airport authorities and freight forwarding companies.

In the area of public purchasing a number of measures and proposals provide a significant opportunity for informatics firms to tackle what have traditionally been closed sectors in national markets. In particular, the extension of the purchasing rules to telecommunications is part of a wider effort to bring in the previously excluded sectors of water, energy, transport and telecommunications. The proposals break new ground in that they will apply to entities operating on the basis of special or exclusive rights granted by Member States, irrespective of their legal status. This means that the purchasers of a state-controlled PTT in one Member State will be treated in a like manner to that of its privatised equivalent in another.

The Commission has also issued proposals to extend the public purchasing rules to the service industries. Initially, they are concentrating on the procurement of software, management consultancy and construction services.

The liberalisation of public procurement was given a boost in February 1987, when the Council of Ministers adopted a decision which requires public purchases to specify OSI (Open Systems Interconnection) standards when purchasing informatics systems.

Broadly speaking, all public sector purchases with a value of over ECU 100,000 should conform to available OSI standards. As central and local government probably account for 10-15 per cent of the market for informatics purchases, this should also act as a stimulus for the use of OSI.

ELECTRONIC DATA INTERCHANGE (EDI)

In searching for areas in which to improve their efficiency and thereby their competitiveness, organisations will need to examine their procedures for dealing with external organisations, such as customers and suppliers. Internationalisation of trade and rapidly changing world markets are causing an increase in the amount of information that has to be exchanged between organisations. The development of systems for inter-company automation are bringing about a fundamental shift in business practice. Foremost amongst these systems is Electronic Data Interchange (EDI) — the most rapidly growing activity in informatics with forecast levels of growth of between 50 per cent and 100 per cent in Europe and the USA.

Electronic Data Interchange eliminates the labour-intensive, lengthy and error-prone process of passing information between corporate computers via paper and postal services; ie orders, invoices, product information, etc. It also makes it possible to add value to, and extract information from, the various business transactions carried out by the organisation. A company can, for example, provide a better service by allowing a customer greater flexibility in placing and changing orders while an audit of EDI transactions will provide better information on a customer's buying pattern.

An EDI system consists of the following three basic components:

Communications Network

This carries the electronic messages securely between different organisations' computers. It is made of the organisation's own private network, third party network suppliers and the public network supplied by telecommunications administrations.

Translation Software

This is required to take raw data from one organisation's computers, condition it for transmission to another organisation's computers and then convert it into the form used in the latter. This software is required because of the variety of computers and applications packages used by different organisations. Data in one computer may not be usable directly by another. The translation software can be installed on one of the organisations' computers or in a central clearing location. The decision on which is the best approach depends on the overall informatics systems of the individual organisations involved and the nature of the transactions between them.

Message Standards

EDI message standards have to be developed because business data is stored in a company's computers in many different formats. Moreover, EDI is used to communicate between many different industries and different sectors of industry in many different countries. Manufacturers communicate with retailers, retailers communicate with financial institutions and so on. A set of agreed message standards enables organisations to communicate in a meaningful fashion without the need to synchronise their internal applications software.

There are a variety of industry bodies producing standards for EDI, such as the Article Numbering Association, The United Nations Economic Commission for Europe, American National Standards Institute and the EDIFACT board. They either produce, promote or oversee the development and deployment of standards.

Most practical implementations of EDI have been focused on intra-industry communications. There are substantial opportunities both within and across industry segments.

Industrial Applications of EDI

The earliest non-financial applications of EDI in Europe were in the automobile manufacturing industry. The ODETTE project was conceived to evaluate whether a system of teletransmission of data between manufacturers and suppliers was possible. ODETTE's focus was, and still is, on the content and structure of the documents passed between the supplier and the manufacturer. The interest generated by ODETTE, and the potential improvement in efficiency it outlined, stimulated practical implementations of EDI. One of the most ambitious projects has been undertaken by Electronic Data Systems on behalf of General Motors, linking them to more than 2000 suppliers across Europe.

The retail industry also developed an early interest in EDI to overcome the extremely high administrative burden imposed by manually processing delivery notes and reconciling them with invoices. In the UK, the Article Numbering Association (ANA) developed the national EDI data standard, TRADACOMS. The TRADACOMS standards group was formed to review the procedure, and the effort to standardise the syntax and content of trading messages opened up the possibility of computer-to-computer communications. The ANA selected the INS (International Network Services Ltd) TRADANET service. TRADANET INTERNATIONAL is a combination of TRADANET in the UK linked to EDI*EXPRESS, the GEIS (General Electric Information Services) service worldwide. The linking of these two services has created the world's largest EDI Community of over 5000 customers.

Banks have been using a form of EDI known as Electronic Funds Transfer (EFT) for some time. Electronic messages are used to move money between accounts in different banks nationally and internationally. Examples are the Bankers Automated Clearing Service in the UK (BACS) and the Society for World Inter-bank Financial Telecommunications (SWIFT). These services use the direct exchange of information between computers owned and operated by banks to move funds from one account to another in a different bank. SWIFT, for instance, connects over 2000 banks in 50 different countries.

EDI also impacts the carriage of goods and people by air, sea, rail and road. For instance, EDI can give manufacturers direct input to airline cargo handling and customs clearance systems. The International Network Services Ltd (INS) has developed software using EDIFACT standards for the exchange of shipping documentation, and reports that their customers find that goods get shipped faster, they gain administrative savings and airfreight consignments can be loaded one day earlier than when previous procedures were used. Thus, EDI improves a company's export efficiency and dramatically changes the role of the Freight Forwarder.

The application of EDI to the movement of people is associated with the need to deal with the escalating number of transactions required to organise an individual's journey; producing tickets for multiple airlines, reserving hotel accommodation and scheduling car hire. Europe's people carriers are competing with each other to develop customer reservation systems. The travel agents who use these systems will demand an EDI approach similar to the system in use by ferry operators who use United Nations Interactive Concept Over Reservation Networks (UNICORN) as a standard.

Future Development of EDI

Whilst EDI offers great scope for increasing the efficiency, speed and accuracy of an organisation's external transactions. It may be worth noting that there are still some limitations to its use that need to be overcome. First, EDI automates inter-company business transactions where an agreement to do business already exists and no further decisions are required on the data which is to be exchanged. This will continue to be the main application although it is technically possible to create systems which perform a function similar to the computer trading systems on the Stock Exchange.

The convenience of conducting business electronically may cause companies to change their suppliers as products become less differentiated by price and performance, and the focus turns to the actual business relationship and how the company is perceived in the marketplace.

It seems likely that most EDI services will be obtained from a third party or value added service provider since the general scope of an EDI implementation is beyond the reach of most organisations' informatics departments. This is borne out by the fact that the successful implementations to date have been carried out by consortia and industry groups. Furthermore, as companies that are in competition for business need to co-operate, independent third parties are able to act as intermediaries to ensure consensus on the communications issues and treat the industry sector evenly.

One of the main issues associated with EDI is the legal aspect. The problem area is where there is a need to exchange a signed document as required by law or commercial practice. EDI cannot be used, as the transmission of electronic signatures is not accepted. However, Barclays Bank introduced a 'Trading Master' service in August 1990, that arranges for payments and remittance advices to be carried out over EDIFACT, thereby making the agreement explicit without the need for a signature.

The remaining issues are standards, technology and changes to companies' business structure. There seems to be a confusing array of bodies developing, promoting and rationalising standards. It is necessary, therefore, to ensure that the EDI project does not become bogged down in this area. The simple pragmatic approach is to use a stable standard if it exists. If the standard is changing, use it but avoid being locked out of the new standard. If there is no standard, set one and have it accepted by an industry body. In general terms, most business transactions will move towards the EDIFACT standard but this should not encourage a strategy of waiting until the standard is stable. By then it will be too late.

EDI is a stable and practical technology. The scope and dimensions of an EDI project, however, involving activity over a broad geography with many independent organisations, requires a great deal of expertise. This means that the project needs to be handled differently from traditional intra-company IT implementations.

EDI implementation will require changes to be made to a company's business structure. Indeed, this is one of the main reasons for its introduction. Several departments within a company may need to be restructured and the distribution of functions rearranged. In particular, the internal DP department may feel that its responsibilities are being encroached upon by third parties, and access to the computers under its charge is being given to 'outsiders'.

The Commission has set up an advisory service on EDI to help companies and industrial sectors co-ordinate their activities so that they can all benefit from trouble-free communications. TEDIS (Trade Electronic Data Interchange Service) encourages interworking and also offers advice on the technical and legal problems involved. Further information is available from:

Robert Wakeling
TEDIS, DG XIII
Rue de la Loi, 200
1049-BRUSSELS
Belgium.

Telephone: 010 322 236 0029 or +322 235 0029, the TEDIS secretariat is on 010 322 235 1936 or +322 235 1936.

SPRINT

The SPRINT (Strategic PRogramme for Innovation and technology Transfer) programme was initiated several years before the negotiations which led to the *Single European Act* and arose from the Commission's long involvement in research. In the late 1970s the Commission became concerned to see better exploitation of the results of Community R&D programmes, and a small department was set up for this purpose. It rapidly became clear that many of the problems connected with the exploitation of research results lay downstream from the research process itself. This lead in 1979 to a Community-wide study on the problems of barriers to innovation, the process by which new or improved goods, processes and services are introduced into the economy.

Although many of the barriers identified are more the concern of national or regional authorities, it became evident that, in a market of continental scale, there were numerous opportunities for trans-national synergies between organisations with complementary innovatory strengths.

It could be, for example, that organisations in different Member States possess complementary technologies, or that one organisation possesses a technology for which another can provide market access. While multinational companies have long been able to exploit transnational synergies, the same cannot be said of many SMEs and the research organisations with which they work. It is those organisations with complementary strengths which are the ultimate target of SPRINT.

The aim of the original SPRINT programme was not to finance particular technological developments, but to set up transnational networks which would enable national or regional organisations already active in innovation and technology transfer, to benefit from the dimension of the Community market.

SPRINT has been managed by the Commission, advised by a committee whose members are nominated by the Member States.

There have been calls for proposals in selected areas, the Community's financial contribution usually being 50 per cent of the total cost of the proposed activity. Participants were intermediaries, such as technology consultants, licensing specialists, venture capitalists, chambers of commerce, industrial research associations, etc, acting on behalf of firms, mainly SMEs, rather than firms themselves.

SPRINT has produced interesting results in the following seven areas:

Venture Capital

One of the first things which was discovered from the earlier study on barriers to innovation was that, in Europe, the venture capital industry was far less developed than in the United States. This represented a major barrier to innovation in the Community.

For a few years, starting in 1980, an annual European conference was held and, given the interest shown, financial support was provided for the setting up of the *European Venture Capital Association (EVCA)*. This is now a self-supporting organisation through which venture capitalists in Europe can establsh contacts and find partners. It has over 150 members drawn from all the Member States, and over 20 associate members outside of the Community. EVCA brings together all the largest, and by far the most important, of the 500 or so venture capital companies in Europe.

Networks for Promoting Technological Agreements between Firms

Under this heading SPRINT has done two things. First, it has contributed to the cost of negotiating over 200 technological co-operation agreements involving about 170 contractors. Secondly, it has helped to launch the association TII (see below). Examples of the results of a few of these agreements are given in the booklet *'Innovating across Europe'*, published by SPRINT in 1988. Firms are not invited to submit proposals directly, but through intermediaries from whom proposals have been submitted in the past, and who are already familiar with the administrative procedures.

Research Organisations

More than 20 collaborative projects involving exchanges of information and experience between Research Associations in the UK and similar bodies in other Member States have been set up. For example, ERA Technology Ltd in Leatherhead is one of five partners in a working group on electrostatic problems. In another example SATRA, the Shoe and Allied Trades Research Association, took part in an exchange of information on the application of computer-aided design and manufacturing to the shoe industry, which involved analogous organisations in nine Member States.

In the field of contract research organisations in the Community, the Commission has instituted a survey which analyses the structure of this area.

Conferences

Extra costs are involved in giving a European dimension to a technological conference, in particular for simultaneous interpretation facilities and bringing invited speakers from other countries. SPRINT has contributed to such costs for about 100 conferences.

Industrial Design

A SPRINT working party on industrial design was set up in 1985, having as its principal aim the promotion of trans-national co-operation in using innovative design to further the competitiveness of SMEs. One of the first results was the award of the *European Community Design Prize* to three winners, one from Denmark, Germany and Italy respectively, at a ceremony in Brussels on 15 February, 1988. They were chosen by an international jury from among 32 competing companies.

Industrial design is still largely a national activity, and there is no industrial infrastructure for design in many European countries. SPRINT intends to play a catalytic role in this area, similar to the role played elsewhere.

Intellectual Property Rights

While the setting up of the European Patent Organisation has undoubtedly been of great benefit, as the steadily increasing use of its services demonstrates, practical problems still remain in the area of intellectual property rights and, in particular, when it comes to defending and exploiting these rights. A working party on innovation and patents has been set up in the framework of SPRINT to examine these problems. One of the results of its work has been the publication of a survey of patent infringement costs covering 18 countries; prepared for the Commission by Professor Bouhu, a European Patent Attorney.

A particular problem in Europe in the field of intellectual property rights is the relative lack of motivation on the part of some scientists and engineers to use the patent system to protect their inventions. This was a theme of PATINNOVA '90, a conference on strategies for the protection of inventions held in Madrid in May 1990, and co-financed by SPRINT.

Innovation in Less Favoured Regions

SPRINT has given support to assist innovation in less favoured regions in the Community by, for example, helping the introduction of robotics into Ireland or by the modernisation of the Portuguese Patent Office.

These are the principal areas that SPRINT has supported. Others receiving attention include university-industry relations (including science parks), quality management, value analysis and establishing links between engineering consultancy bodies.

For a long time in most industralised countries public funding to promote innovation has mainly taken the form of financial support for R&D projects. Too often, people concerned with public R&D have ignored the obstacles to the subsequent dissemination of new technologies through manufacture and marketing into the economy. It is these obstacles which, in a Community-wide context, SPRINT is trying to overcome.

The Commission has presented proposals for a new five-year SPRINT programme under three lines of action:

The European innovation services infrastructure

This is the area covered by the original SPRINT programme outlined above, and which the Commission feels needs to be consolidated.

Pilot projects for intra-Community technology transfer

This will involve providing support of various kinds for trans-national pilot projects with industrial participation, involving the application of generic technologies to industrial sectors in less developed or declining regions in the Community. The emphasis will be on reducing the risks associated with the proposed technology transfer (through appropriate studies and evaluations) for the firms concerned to commit their resources with confidence.

Improving the innovative environment through a better understanding of the process involved

The central problem is to arrive at a more exact understanding of the innovation process, so that the Member States and the Commission can keep track better of what is happening and take appropriate action in time. For many years it was considered adequate to measure levels of public expenditure on R&D. That approach measures only one of the inputs to the innovation process, whereas it is no less necessary to measure the output. In the United States there is the National Science Foundation's publication *Science Indicators*, but so far little exists at Community level.

More information about SPRINT is given in the DG XIII quarterly newsletter, *Innovation & Technology Transfer*.

For further information contact:

DG XIII/C/1
Batiment Jean Monnet
Plateau de Kirchberg, B4/091
2920-LUXEMBOURG.

Telephone: 010 352 43 01 33 51 or + 352 43 01 33 51

TECHNOLOGY INNOVATION INFORMATION

TII is short for the European Association for the Transfer of Technologies, Innovation and Industrial Information — the European association of the innovation support professions. Its aims are:

—   to promote their services and make them more widely known and used by other firms;

—   to facilitate European co-operation between innovation support professions and to help them, so that their client firms benefit from the large internal Community market;

— to provide training in innovation support methods and encourage high professional standards;

— to represent the interests of innovation support professions at a European level.

TII is a non-profit making association (*association sans but lucratif*) under Luxembourg law. Founded with the initial financial support of SPRINT, TII is committed to achieving financial autonomy in the medium term.

TII provides the following services:

TII Focus

The Association's quarterly newsletter carries information on TII and members' activities, and news of Community and other initiatives. Special supplements give members advance warning of new initiatives, invitations to tender, etc. TII's members are, therefore, among the first to know of new initiatives in innovation and technology. Individual advice is available to members wishing to apply for particular programmes. These include SPRINT which in 1989-93 is launching a wide range of measures to promote innovation support in Europe.

The TII Directory of Members

This is revised annually and profiles the services of individual members. It makes members known to one another and to a wide audience of professionals and firms.

The TII European Innovation Directory

Based on the Association's 9000-strong file of innovation support organisations in Europe, the Directory is a unique 'Who's Who' giving prominence to TII members and targeted for world-wide distribution.

TII Training Seminars

Experienced   professionals   introduce   members   to   proven techniques of innovation and support. Current topics in the short (two-day) seminar series are: technology auditing, marketing techniques for innovative products, innovation financed by venture capital, marketing of information services, negotiation and legal protection of technology transfer. Basic training seminars (one week) for new entrants to the innovation support professions provide an overview of key methods and practices.

TII Contact Services

TII arranges two-day group visits to meet the innovation support community in selected regions of the Community. Individual staff exchanges can be arranged for up to three months; visits to technology fairs for heads of firms can be laid on. These services are supported by the SPRINT programme.

TII's Technology Opportunity Exchange

An exclusive service has been developed through which members can send out carefully screened technology questionnaires from their firms.

The TII Code of Professional Conduct

This Code establishes clear minimum rules of professional ethics which are binding on all members and provides a 'label of quality' which assists members when marketing their services.

   TII membership is open generally to all organisations involved in innovation support including:

—   innovation and technology management consultants;

—   universities and technical institutes;

—   contract research organisations;

—   science parks, innovation centres and business schools;

—   venture capitalists and financial institutions;

— large industrial firms;

— licence brokers and intellectual property advisors;

— chambers of commerce and trade;

— local and regional governments;

— regional development bodies;

— government ministries and agencies;

— engineering and design consultants;

— information brokers, database operators and technology publishers;

— organisation and management consultants;

— technology and trade fair organisers.

Full membership is available to organisations whose principal activity is the provision of innovation support services to firms. Associate membership is open to organisations with an involvement in innovation support but which do not directly supply services to firms or for whom the supply of such services is not their principal activity. Full and Associate Membership is restricted to organisations which operate in one or more Member States of the Community.

Affiliate Membership is available to innovation support organisations in non-Community countries which are signatories of scientific, technical or industrial co-operation agreements with the Community, and which have been accepted as eligible for membership by the Annual General Meeting of the Association. These countries include: Cyprus, Finland, Iceland, Leichtenstein, Malta, Norway, Sweden, Switzerland, Turkey and Yugoslavia.

Members may be native or naturalised Europeans, and work in businesses incorporated under public or private law, or which are of mixed public-private status. Applications for membership are assessed by the Association's Board of Management. All categories of members have full access to the Association's services but the voting rights of Associate and Affiliate Members are limited.

Annual membership subscriptions are calculated on a sliding scale (ECU 265-3,150 in 1989) according to the size of the member organisation. The average subscription is about ECU 600. Benefactor members make discretionary additional contributions.

Further information is available from:

> M Michel Duhamel
> Secretary General
> The European Association for the Transfer of
>   Technologies Innovation and Industrial Information
> Rue des Capucins, 3,
> 1313-LUXEMBOURG.

> Telephone: 010 352 46 30 35 or +352 46 30 35

BC-NET

BC-NET (Business Co-operation NETwork) is a system that aims to help one company find another so that they can enter into co-operation in the fields of international finance, commerce and technical collaboration (including sharing of technologies and direct sub-contracting). It is particularly directed towards SMEs.

It is based upon existing 'business advisory' organisations of which there are 400 distributed throughout the Community countries and connected with each other by the BC-NET communications network. Business advisory organisations help SMEs develop their business: they may be private consultants, chambers of commerce, banks, business agencies, solicitors, regional development agencies or agencies specialising in business sectors, etc.

In BC-NET terms, a business advisor is a private or public body whose purpose is to help companies, particularly SMEs, to formulate co-operation details and to conduct the search for another matching company. A business advisor must be sufficiently well acquainted with his clients to make qualitative judgements on their ability to offer (or request) collaboration.

When an SME company seeks to collaborate with a company in another Member State, it first turns to its business advisors who formulate the request as a 'co-operation profile' which can then be sent to BC-NET either by post, telex, fax or telecommunications.

BC-NET stores all offers in its data bank and requests are matched with those offers. If the data bank contains appropriate matches, immediate answers are sent both to the originator of the request and to the originator of the offer. Should the data bank not contain any appropriate match, the profile can, if the company so wishes, be automatically distributed as a 'flash profile' to those BC-NET users in the geographical area covered by the request.

BC-NET was introduced in 1988 on an experimental basis for two years. During that period more than 20,000 co-operation profiles have been received and dealt with. On the basis of results obtained during the experimental period, the Commission is formulating proposals for a post-experiment BC-NET which address the following points:

— improvement of the system, particularly the nomenclatures;

— new applications and developments;

— telecommunications methods;

— extension of the BC-NET system to non-community states, particularly those in EFTA;

— the possibility of entrusting the management of the BC-NET system to the advisors who are using it (without the Commission losing control).

For further information contact:

Theodoros Kallianos
DG XIII — BC-NET
Commmission of the European Communities
Rue de la Loi, 200 (ARLN)
1049-BRUSSELS, Belgium

Telephone: 010 322 235 8591 or +322 235 8591

4 Collaborative Programmes in Research and Development

INTRODUCTION

The Community has recognised the need to promote collaborative programmes in research and development (R&D) with the twofold aim of raising the base level of technology throughout the Community and to encourage collaboration both between organisations in different Member States and between the different sectors, particularly industry and education. It is expected that collaboration in pre-competitive R&D will lead to a development of mutual respect and, hence, to collaboration in production, marketing and sales, with the resulting benefits from the economies of scale.

This chapter gives an outline of most of the major programmes with sufficient detail for the reader to decide if his or her organisation might be interested in participating.

THE FRAMEWORK PROGRAMME

The Framework Programme is the grouping of R&D initiatives and programmes that have been launched by the Commission. During 1989, the Commission reviewed the status of the Programme, its success, and the requirements for R&D within the Community for the next five years. The stimulus for this examination was the mid-term review of the Framework Programme which resulted in various analyses and studies, eg the *First Report on the State of Science and Technology (December 1988)*, and the evaluation report drawn up by five independent experts (June 1989). From considerations brought to light by such reports, the Commission submitted to the Council of Ministers a proposal for a new Framework Programme to cover the years 1990-1994. This was not just a simple revision of the current programme limited to the years 1990-1991. It enabled the Commission to make essential strategic adjustments to the proposed programme that would have been more difficult with a simple revision of the current Framework Programme.

The proposed changes took into account the following considerations:

— The rate of technological change is accelerating;

— There is a continuing need to strengthen the competitiveness of European industry to combat increased international competition.

— The Single Act has given new directions and new impetus for R&D.

The previous Framework Programme was organised under eight headings and had a budget of about ECU 3 billion. The eight headings and budgets were:

— Information society;

— Energy;

— Modernisation of industrial sectors;

— Quality of life;

— Biological resources;

— European science and technology;

— Marine sciences;

— Scientific co-operation with developing countries.

The new Programme has been regrouped into six activities under three main headings:

—   Enabling Technologies covering Information and Communication Technologies; and Industrial and Material Technologies;

—   Management of Natural Resources covering Environment; Life Sciences and Technologies; and Energy;

—   Management of Intellectual Resources covering Human Capital and Mobility.

The Commission states that this grouping gives pertinence, concentration and flexibility of management for Community activity.

The Programme was approved by the Council and the Commission launched six specific programmes corresponding to these six new activity areas. This does not necessarily imply new activities; rather the concentration of the programmes leads to an increase in the size of projects. This, however, should not prejudice the need to involve smaller organisations and academic institutions.

The Commission requested a budget of ECU 7.7 billion spread over the five years of 1990-1994, distributed as shown in Table 4.1. The previous (1987-1991) Framework Programme had a budget of ECU 3.1 billion. In the event, on 23 April 1990, the Council approved a budget of ECU 5.7 billion split ECU 2500 million for 1990-92 and ECU 3200 million for 1993-94; the latter will not be for new projects but for the continuation of projects begun in 1990-92. The allocation for informatics is ECU 2221 million — ECU 1352 million for information technology, ECU 489 million for communications technology and ECU 380 million for telematics systems. The division between years for informatics is ECU 974 million for 1990-92 and ECU 1247 million for 1993-94.

Because of the growing importance of micro-electronics and advanced networks for interconnections between information systems, it is intended that these will be given an appreciable increase in support at the expense of more traditional areas. Another area that is of interest to the informatics community is the predicted shortage of skilled young researchers. It is intended that a concerted effort will be made on the management of intellectual resources.

Areas of ECU Budget distribution 1990-1994	ECU millions
ENABLING TECHNOLOGIES	
Information and communications technologies	3,000
Industrial and materials technologies	1,200
MANAGEMENT OF NATURAL RESOURCES	
Environment	700
Life sciences and technologies	1,100
Energy	1,000
MANAGEMENT OF INTELLECTUAL RESOURCES	
Human capital and mobility	700
TOTAL	7,700

Table 4.1 Spread of ECU Budget 1990-1994

The only true measure of the effectiveness of these programmes will be success in bringing to the marketplace the products and services which incorporate the results of the projects. The VALUE (VALorisation and Utilisation for Europe) programme was introduced, therefore, to provide a range of services to organisations involved in Community research programmes to help protect, exploit and disseminate the results of their work. It also has a sub-programme concerned with the creation of a computer communications infrastructure. The budget is ECU 38 million over the four years 1989-1992. Further information is available from:

Jean-Noel Durvy
DG XIII/C
Commission of the European Communities
Batiment Jean Monnet B4/107
2920-LUXEMBOURG.

Telephone: 010 352 4301-3453 or +352 4301-3453.

It is worth noting the areas in which the Commission indicates that it will direct the programmes.

Information Technologies

There is an indication that the research within the ESPRIT programme (see below) will be directed towards prototypes and multi-supplier systems. The following areas (which are already technology areas within ESPRIT) will receive attention:

— Micro-electronics: Particular attention will be given to integrated circuits in conjunction with the Joint European Submicron Silicon Initiative (JESSI);

— Peripherals: The action will favour the production of reliable, low cost, mass-produced input/output and storage peripherals;

— Software: The proposed programme will continue to develop systems and tools aimed at improving productivity in software production;

— IT applied to industrial engineering: The programme will continue to examine ways of optimising the use of advanced CAD/CAM systems. This will be concentrated in strategically important industrial sectors.

Communication Technologies

In parallel with the continued development within RACE (see below) of an integrated broadband network, the new Programme will have objectives of developing intelligent, reliable and secure networks, as well as value added and profitable services. These will have to be adapted to developing user needs as the users themselves become more sophisticated and aware of the available facilities. There is, for example, recognition of the growing demand for mobile telephone facilities and the need to integrate these into networks if they are to be effective and widely used. The requirements of private and leisure use are also to be taken into account, not just those of business. The development of the technology and the provision of successive generations of networks, means that the user needs to be able to migrate easily through the generations. To meet this, the following actions are proposed:

— development of intelligent networks using optical communications and artificial intelligence;

— work on mobile communications with special attention to their security;

— research into image communication, including HDTV (High Definition TeleVision). Special efforts are required to integrate image communication into other networks to produce multimedia communications;

— service engineering research, including work on architectures and software.

This will be accompanied by other actions aimed at improving the security of communication systems. Also proposed is the development of technologies for verification and testing of hardware, software and systems.

Development of Telematic Systems in Areas of General Interest

The Commission has started programmes using communication networks in certain application areas:

— DELTA Distance Learning (see Chapter 5);

— AIM Application of IT in Medicine (see below);

— DRIVE Transport (see below).

The Programme points the way for the use of communication networks in other areas such as environmental protection, access to rural areas, customs (and excise), justice and social security. The Commission envisages that full development of telematics systems in the above applications areas will take place outside the Programme, but that preparatory R&D work, including language research, engineering and pilot experiments, could take place within. Eventually the Commission expects that there will be a European Nervous System (ENS) integrating all of these applications. The ENS will be particularly valuable in replacing border controls whilst still enabling the authorities in Member States to combat drug trafficking, terrorism and tax fraud.

Other sections of the Programme will have implications for informatics, but they are primarily concerned with other matters such as Industrial and Materials technologies, Management of Natural resources (Environment, Life Sciences and Technologies, and Energy).

The problem of the shortage of researchers with appropriate skills is also catered for. The Programme addresses issues of mobility of young graduate researchers across the Community, and also the problem of provision of training in knowledge of basic sciences and its application to technologies.

THE ESPRIT PROGRAMME

Background

Within the general Framework Programme the most important programme in informatics is the ESPRIT (European Strategic Programme for Research and development in Information Technology) Programme. The first phase of this programme, ESPRIT I, started in 1984. The total R&D efforts amounted to ECU 1500 million, half of which was borne by the Community budget, the other half by the participants in the programme.

The programme is implemented by collaborative, precompetitive research and development projects carried out across national frontiers by Community companies, research institutes and universities. Under ESPRIT I, 226 projects were launched, each involving at least two independent industrial partners from different Member States. At its peak, 3000 engineers and scientists from 420 independent organisations were working full-time on ESPRIT projects.

ESPRIT has the following three objectives:

— to provide the European IT industry with the basic technologies to meet the competitive requirements of the
   1990s;

— to promote European industrial co-operation in IT;

— to pave the way for standards.

The priority areas in ESPRIT I were micro-electronics (to
develop the Community's capability for manufacturing
integrated circuits), software (the critical, and increasingly costly,
component of informatics systems) and open systems (to permit
the interoperability of equipment from different suppliers).

Over 100 of the projects have produced significant results,
either in the form of products or services, or as potential
international standards. For example, the OMEGA expert system
shell which is now in use in Europe, the USA and Japan. Another
example is the 'Supernode' machine, the result of a project aimed
at the development of low-cost workstations with a performance
in the region of 380 Mflops at a cost of about ECU 200,000. The
machine is based on the T800 transputer, which was developed
within the project, together with a VLSI non-blocking switching
element which allows full interconnection of the processing
elements. The architecture can be either statically or dynamically
configured. Prototype machines were demonstrated in 1987
running applications covering real-time image processing and
CAD (Computer Aided Design).

The Supernode machine could provide a major breakthrough
in the area of high performance workstations; it is clearly a major
market opportunity since it would appear that this machine has
a performance/cost ratio three or four times better than its
competitors.

Although these results and the other 30 or so like them are important, particular mention should be made of three key results.

Software Technology

In Software Technology the results of the Portable Common Tool
Environment (PCTE) projects are having a significant impact on

the tool and user interface specifications for Integrated Project Support Environments. In 1985, after a major review of the ESPRIT Software Technology programme, it was decided to make the PCTE interfaces the glue for the whole of the Software Technology sub-area. This decision provided a focus for many of the results emerging from the projects; a coherent set of results is now available which provides initial prototypes of real software factories. The PCTE interfaces have now been adopted by a number of programmes in Europe, both civil and defence, and products are on the market which support these interfaces. The interface specifications themselves are under the control of an independent Interface Management Board and have just entered the ECMA standardisation process. Environments supporting the PCTE interfaces are now available free of charge to participants of all Community R&D programmes and to European universities. This is an area in which European technological leadership is giving a major advantage to European industry. A regular 'PCTE Newsletter' is published and further information is available from the PIMB (PCTE Interface Management Board) whose Secretary is:

> Werner Wohlschlegel
> Commission of the European Communities
> Avenue d'Auderghem, 45
> 1040-BRUSSELS
> Belgium.
>
> Telephone: 010 322 236 0257 or +322 236 0257.

Office Systems

In the Office Systems area of the programme, the Office Document Architecture project has also resulted in important industrial standards. Automatic interchange of a range of different document types has been demonstrated between machines from different companies. The architecture specification has already been adopted as an ECMA standard, and is currently progressing through the ISO process. In all, 11 of the office systems projects are having an influence on more than 16 standards working groups, in areas such as open distributed architectures, office document formats and man-machine interfaces.

Computer Integrated Manufacturing

Computer Integrated Manufacturing is another area where European industry is making significant progress. The objective of defining protocols for inter-operability between factory equipment has been given particular attention by the automobile and aerospace industries, and the General Motors initiative has been particularly visible. But of all the initiatives, the ESPRIT Communication Network for Manufacturing Applications (CNMA) project was the first to produce working prototypes conforming to the emerging standards. Three industrial pilot plants have been installed, one by British Aerospace for use on the Airbus A320 wing assembly plant in Salisbury, the second by BMW at their Regensburg plant for their new convertible (this particular installation required 35 Km of optical fibre and has 600 connection points all communicating using the CNMA protocols), and the third pilot plant was installed by Aeritalia.

To judge from the successes achieved in the first phase, ESPRIT is, without any doubt, an excellent illustration of what Europeans can do through co-operation, given an appropriate framework. Three major breakthroughs are clear.

1. The creation of a European technology community based on the association of researchers from industry and academia who have together carried out well-designed practical projects, developed mutual confidence, experienced the pride that comes from joint successes, and learnt that co-operation between people of different nationalities, cultures, education and language is not only possible, but fruitful.

2. ESPRIT has produced tangible results which hold out encouraging prospects for the future production of innovating processes, products and services.

3. The direct role played by ESPRIT in the preparation of standards, and its indirect role in the creation of new industrial structures and in the launching of other co-operative initiatives, such as RACE and Basic Research in Industrial Technologies in Europe (BRITE).

The reasons for this success lie in the determination of the industrialists and scientists involved to succeed, the strategic nature and stringency of the choices made and the co-ordination and consistency of the technical, economic and political initiatives taken by the Community.

Review of ESPRIT I

In October 1988, a Review Board was established under the chairmanship of Dr A E Pannenborg, retired Vice-Chairman of the Board of N V Philips, to:

—   assess the extent to which ESPRIT I was achieving its objectives;

—   determine the effects of the programme;

—   assess the need for any changes affecting ESPRIT or future IT-related Community programmes.

The Review Board found that in the majority of projects trans-European co-operation had been a success and resulted in significant benefits for the participants. There have been direct benefits of being able to cover a wider range of research topics more quickly by sharing the work and the results with the project partners.

As a result of ESPRIT, Europe's technological base has improved its techniques, facilities and human resources. Good work has been done on international standards. Links between industry and universities have been strengthened and, transnationally, have often been created for the first time. Managerial awareness of the strategic importance of informatics has been heightened.

The Review Board found the management of ESPRIT generally satisfactory and smooth, with sensible procedures. Nevertheless, they felt that the management could be improved in a number of respects. The handling of contract negotiation and the speed of payments were criticised. The Commission was also perceived to have failed in making the results of projects available to those working on other projects.

The Review Board pointed out that the greater the number of partners the harder a project is to manage. It is difficult to identify distinct complementary roles between several partners, and visits to each participant's premises becomes time-consuming. For these reasons, the Review Board recommended that for future programmes the number of partners in any project should not, except for standards projects, rise above six.

ESPRIT II

ESPRIT II was launched in 1988 with a budget of ECU 3200 million — again, half of this money was provided from Community funds and the other half by industrial participants. This is estimated to represent about 5 per cent of the R&D expenditure of the European informatics industry.

ESPRIT II concentrates on three main areas:

1. *Micro-electronics and peripherals* — in particular, emphasis is being given to the facilities for the efficient production of 'Application Specific Integrated Circuits'.

2. *Information processing systems* — this programme will concentrate on full system design, complexity management, using results from previous projects where software technology has been integrated with advanced information processing technologies such as knowledge engineering, advanced architectures and signal processing.

3. *IT application technologies* — this covers computer integrated manufacturing, integrated information systems and informatics application support systems (man/machine interface, workstations, distributed systems, storage and retrieval systems).

ESPRIT is open to companies, academic institutions and research bodies irrespective of size or whether they are public or private. The basic level of Community support is 50 per cent of all allowable costs, although universities and research institutions can opt for 100 per cent of additional expenditure as an alternative. As a rule, each project must include industrial companies from at least two Member States.

Two categories of project are supported in ESPRIT. Type A projects are aimed at specific strategic goals with well-defined objectives, requiring substantial resources and large teams. Some 70 per cent of ESPRIT funds are allocated for projects of this kind, usually requiring ECU 10 million or more. Type B projects are smaller, more speculative, research-oriented projects for which the work programme only suggests general themes.

Management of ESPRIT is a co-operative effort between the Commission, which undertakes all day-to-day organisational tasks, the 'Round Table' of the eleven largest European informatics firms, an ESPRIT Advisory Board and the ESPRIT Management Committee (consisting of Government representatives from Member States).

The programme is organised on a regular cycle. Submissions are invited through calls for proposals which are published in the Official Journal of the European Communities. These calls are based on a Work Programme, published in advance which sets out the detailed project requirements. The notice period for calls is relatively short, about three months from official notification. It can take substantially longer than this to put together a collaborative project of the quality necessary to succeed in what is a very competitive process. It is essential, therefore, to keep in touch with the ESPRIT Office to obtain advance information about calls for proposals that are in the pipeline. The head of the ESPRIT Office is:

> Ian Collison
> ESPRIT
> DG XIII
> Rue de la Loi, 200
> B-1049 BRUSSELS
> Belgium.

> Telephone: 010 322 236 2067 or +322 236 2067;
> For general enquiries: 010 322 235 7666 or + 322 235 7666.

RACE

RACE stands for Research and development of Advanced Communication technologies in Europe. The RACE programme has been set up by the Community to establish the infrastructure for communications throughout Europe by introducing Integrated Broadband Communication (IBC).

Integrated Broadband Communication is a system of terminals, switches, computers and satellites that are linked together to handle telephone, television and data transmission in an integrated way. Broadband means that it will have a large transmission capacity to handle several information channels simultaneously.

Since one of the aims is reduction of cost to the user, new services such as videotelephony, home banking and shopping will become economically possible. IBC will open up new opportunities for home entertainment with a large choice of television channels and online access to video libraries. IBC will make distance less important and enable more people to work at home, or in nearby local offices, thus reducing the need to commute into large cities. It will bring remote and rural areas more closely in touch and thereby make it possible for them to share fully in the prosperity of Europe.

The integration of the services depends on using the same equipment for all applications and avoiding a proliferation of new and potentially incompatible devices. This requires that all communications should be transmitted in the same form. Thus, all signals will be converted into digital form, as music is on compact disc. Several countries have already made a start by combining digital voice and data transmission in an Integrated Services Digital Network (ISDN).

Co-operation

The convergence of telecommunications, computing and new information services makes it essential that there should be co-operation between national telecommunications administrations, the electronics industry and the service providers. The establishment of a single European market in 1992, and the liberalisation of competition in providing telecommunications equipment and services, reinforces the need for collaboration in the development of standards.

Eleven telecommunications administrations, 89 universities and research organisations and over 230 companies are involved in international consortia, each of which is tackling one or more of 107 tasks. About 2000 people are collaborating in 85 projects. Organisations from 11 of the 12 Member States are involved. Major US companies established in Europe, such as IBM and AT&T, also participate. Links with EFTA countries have been established — 32 organisations from Austria, Finland, Norway, Sweden and Switzerland have joined in with 39 of the consortia.

Links with the European standardisation bodies (ETSI, CEN/CENELEC, SPAG and EBU, described in Chapter 6) ensure that the results of the programme are carried through into the definition of standards.

Aims and Objectives

The aims of the RACE programme are:

—   to create a climate of co-operation between telecommunications administrations and industry;

—   to make a major contribution to the introduction of IBC Community-wide services in 1995, taking into account the evolving ISDN and national strategies;

—   to promote the competitiveness of the Community's telecommunications industry, operators and service providers.

These broad and laudable aims have been fleshed out a little more in the following statement of objectives:

—   to promote the Community's telecommunications industry;

—   to enable European network operators to compete under the best possible conditions;

— to enable a critical number of Member States to introduce commercially viable IBC services in 1995;

— to allow service providers to improve cost-performance and introduce new services;

— to make new services available at a cost and on a timetable at least as favourable as elsewhere;

— to support the formation of a single European market for equipment and services;

— to contribute to regional development by allowing less developed regions to benefit from telecommunications developments.

The RACE programme contains elements of basic research, and extends up to market-oriented development. It creates opportunities for innovation in product design, development and manufacture, and reflects the realities of telecommunications operations, equipment manufacture, the need for evolution from current systems and the importance of cost. It is also concerned with making the equipment and services easy to use.

RACE is not concerned with technology as such: it is a carefully planned programme of research and development aimed at producing the right technology, at the right price and at the right time, for well specified applications.

Programme Structure

The programme consists of three concurrent parts:

— IBC development and implementation;

— IBC technology R&D;

— Functional integration.

IBC development and integration

A careful investigation is being undertaken on the integration of advanced telecommunications, interactive data services and entertainment services. Satellites will play a key role in long distance links and in the distribution of television programmes. The teams working on this part of the project are on the lookout for opportunities to introduce new services and applications.

The approach is systematic. First, users' requirements are being determined. Then, specifications are being drawn up for the network as a whole. This will be followed by a series of specifications stating what each component of the network is expected to do. Finally, a model of the network will be constructed to check that the components all work together and provide the services required by the users.

IBC Technologies

Having specified what each component is to do, R&D is needed to find ways of doing it. Technology is changing rapidly and the transmission techniques will be required to keep pace with high-speed computers that will be linked together by the IBC. Thus, digitisation of sounds and images will be essential.

The two main methods of sending information are by circuit-switching and by packet switching. In circuit switching a complete path is established between the transmitter and the receiver of the information before the information is passed — as in telephone circuits. In packet switching the information is collected together in small packets and passed from node to node of the network. Only those nodes on the network leading to the intended receiver of the information will need to pass it on, the others ignore it. Packet-switching is, therefore, analogous to sending a letter through the post.

A new method of transmission is being investigated for the IBC known as Asynchronous Transfer Mode (ATM). This combines the advantages of circuit and packet-switching, is flexible and makes the best use of transmission capacity.

The technology for using optical fibres already exists but the various switches and connection equipment are too expensive for general applications. This part of the programme is particularly concerned with reducing the cost, as well as developing novel systems and components. The systems being studied include direct transmission, ie shining a beam of light, and coherent transmission through optical fibres. For the components, work is being carried out on advanced lasers, devices for discriminating between light of different frequencies, switches, amplifiers, connectors and joints.

Work is in progress to reduce the volume of data that needs to be transmitted for video signals. Many pictures change only slowly compared with the renewal of the image on the screen. It is possible, therefore, to transmit the change, which require much less data to be sent, without losing any of the information content of the message. Similar techniques can also be used for voice transmission in digital form, and even in binary coded data using advanced mathematical techniques.

Functional Integration

As the name of this part of the RACE programme implies, it is looking at the way all the various services can be brought together and, of course, the way a network is put together depends on how it will be used. The main thrust has been, therefore, on pilot projects for new applications.

Some examples of the services that IBC will make widely available exist on a limited scale. Video-conferencing can be carried out between Brussels, Luxembourg, Strasbourg and national capitals; interactive video-services are available to over 200,000 French homes connected by optical fibre in the '122 cities' project; over 18,000 Km of optical fibre has been installed in West Berlin to test broadband digital services.

Applications in manufacturing industries and in data and video communication in a hospital started in 1988. Developments in banking and finance, printing and publishing, and insurance started in 1989.

The main new development on the domestic front is high definition television (HDTV) which will permit the use of larger screens; text will be easier to read and digital quality sound will be available in a range of languages. In addition, powerful data-retrieval and display facilities will be provided for all subscribers.

In businesses, high-speed colour fax (facsimile transmission) will become possible, and large flat panel colour displays will enhance video-telephony and video-conferencing. Higher resolution colour visual display units will prove of value in computer-aided design, and electronic communication between design offices and production facilities will speed up the manufacturing process.

IBC will make collaboration within Europe much easier, without the expense and fatigue of travel. Businesses will be able to operate more easily outside major cities.

When?

The RACE programme is ambitious, and there are risks in predicting when the results of the research will be available. Much of the technology exists, however, and has been applied on a small scale. The main difficulty will be in managing the evolution from where we are to where we want to be. Moreoever, it will not be easy to gain consensus on all proposals. Ironically, the less developed regions will probably be first to introduce IBC since they start from scratch and having nothing to replace. They are also the areas with most to gain from being connected up to their more prosperous neighbours.

Firm decisions have already been taken on the strategy for the introduction and evolution of the first IBC network. By mid-1990, a set of proposals should have been prepared for defining the system architecture. These will have to be tested and verified in all EC countries. Final agreement on the architecture is expected to be reached by the end of 1991.

The one firm date given in all RACE documentation is that the IBC will be introduced as a commercial service in 1995. The plans to attain this seem reasonable. Then Nation will be able to speak unto Nation — and communicate images, and data — all at a reasonable cost.

Further information on RACE is available from Jurgen Rosenbaum at the usual address for DG XIII. Telephone: 010 322 235 9235 or + 322 235 9235; general enquiries: 010 322 236 3443/3410 or +322 236 3443/3410.

AIM

The Council decision to establish the AIM (Advanced Informatics in Medicine) programme was announced in the 'Official Journal of the European Communities' on 4 November 1988, but it had been bouncing round the decision making bodies for several months before that. The proposals had to be submitted by noon on 14 February, 1989 so it was essential for applicants to have done their spadework before the official announcement. The Commission announced the results of the Phase 1 projects evaluation in September 1989.

The theme of AIM is the sustained improvement of health care in the Community within economically acceptable limits by exploiting the potential of informatics being applied to it. Given this general objective, AIM has the following goals, namely to:

— improve the quality, accessibility and flexibility of health care;

— increase the effectiveness of patient care, bringing about a reduction of costs;

— contribute to the establishment of minimum standards and common functional specifications;

— contribute to agreed codes of good practice, protection of privacy and reliability;

— stimulate collaboration and concentration of effort in the analysis of the requirements and opportunities of medical and bio-informatics and its application;

— contribute to the common adaptation of the regulatory framework to advances in the nature of health care.

The funds approved were 20 million ECU and an indicative allocation of these funds was:

— Improvement of the effectiveness of public and private actions — ECU 4.80 million.

- Development of a common conceptual framework for collaboration.

— Strengthening Europe's position in the application of information technology and telecommunications to health care — ECU 10.70 million.

- Medical informatics environment;

- Data structures and medical records;

- Communication and functional integration;

- Integration of knowledge-based systems into health care;

- Advanced instrumentation, equipment and services for health care and medical research environment;

— Creation of an environment favourable to the rapid introduction and appropriate application of medical and bio-informatics (MBI) in health care — ECU 2.25 million;

— Administrative and personnel costs — ECU 2.25 million.

Further information can be obtained from Neils Rossing in the Commission. Telephone: 010 322 235 5383 or +322 235 5383; general enquiries: 010 322 235 2706/8 or +322 236 2076/8.

DRIVE

DRIVE stands for *Dedicated Road Infrastructure for Vehicle Safety in Europe* and has three aims:

— to improve road safety;

— to improve road transport efficiency;

— to reduce environmental pollution.

These aims are being pursued through a programme of applying informatics (Road Transport Informatics or RFI) to vehicles and the traffic support system.

Prototype systems are being produced and evaluated. The projects include communication between vehicles and traffic control centres, route guidance systems, incident detection, systems for monitoring traffic congestion, parking management, pollution monitoring and collision avoidance.

The integration of public and private transport, including commercial fleet services, is being studied. The pattern of use of highways and possible changes to increase their capacity is also under investigation.

Further details are available from Fotis Karamitsos in DG XIII. Telephone: 010 322 236 2476 or +322 236 2476; general enquiries: 010 322 236 1130/2481 or +322 236 1130/2481.

COST

COST (European Co-operation in the field of Scientific and Technical Research) is an informal organisation set up by a European Ministerial Conference in 1971 which provides a mechanism for European collaboration in R&D and complements the Community's programmes. It operates through a series of co-operative projects which enable a variable number of participants to mount a joint attack on research areas of common interest and to exchange the results amongst themselves.

Participating countries are free to choose in which projects they are going to participate, and control their own research contribution and financial arrangements. Each project is managed by a Management Committee consisting of experts from all the participating countries.

The overall management of COST is the responsibility of the COST Senior Officials Committee (CSO), which is composed of representatives from the Member States and the Commission. The Commission provides the Secretariats for individual projects unless the participants agree to administer the work themselves.

COST does not fund projects though it does maintain a small central fund based on contributions by the participating countries which helps to pay the costs of coordination activity during the preparatory phase of projects.

There are 19 Member States in COST; the 12 Member States of the European Community and Austria, Finland, Norway, Sweden, Switzerland, Turkey and Yugoslavia. All the Member States have equal rights and, therefore, any state is entitled to submit a proposal for a new COST project. Extension of the membership was considered by the Council which recognised the advantages of opening COST projects to "participation from non-COST states, in particular from other European states on a case-by-case basis where there is a clear scientific justification and where the benefits are mutual." (Official Journal of the European Communities, C171/01; 6.7.89).

Telecommunications is one of the active areas in COST. There is little activity on informatics — probably due to the great deal of activity under ESPRIT.

For further information contact:

COST Secretariat
Council of the European Communities
Rue de la Loi, 170
1048-BRUSSELS
Belgium.

Telephone: 010 322 234 6111 or +322 234 6111.

EUREKA

EUREKA is not a Community programme but a framework for industry-led projects aimed at producing high technology goods and services to compete in world markets against the US and Japan. These projects are normally downstream of, and complementary to, Community programmes.

There are 19 participating countries including the 12 Member States plus Austria, Iceland, Switzerland, Sweden, Norway, Turkey and Finland. The Commission itself is also a EUREKA participant. Activities are undertaken in a wide range of advanced technologies such as information technology, telecommunications, robotics, materials, advanced manufacturing, biotechnology, lasers, etc.

Projects are proposed and run by firms and research institutes, and bureaucracy is kept to a minimum with governments providing a project information 'matchmaking' network and market opening measures. These allow project participants to seek political support for removal of relevant market barriers (eg incompatible standards or regulatory regimes). Public funding is at the discretion of national governments; most provide up to 50 per cent. Examples of projects are High Definition Television and the FAMOS project in flexible automated assembly.

For further information contact:

> EUREKA Secretariat
> 19H, Avenue des Arts, Bte 3
> 1040-BRUSSELS
> Belgium.

> Telephone: 010 322 217 0030 or +322 217 0030.

PROTEAS

Proteas (PROTotypes European Access System) was introduced by DG XIII in August 1988 to provide information for European companies about research projects with commercial potential that have not yet reached the marketplace. At present it is restricted to the informatics areas. The database is one of the ways in which the Commission is trying to ensure that the Community derives greater benefit from its research projects, some of which are funded under the ESPRIT programme.

The specification for PROTEAS is:

— an online database of potentially exploitable developments as yet untested in the market;

— accessible using public data networks from anywhere within Europe;

— searchable by subscribers using combinations of keywords and free text to identify developments of potential interest within defined technical boundaries;

— information is collected through the help of entry questionnaires, from various points within Member States and the service will be properly promoted as it will depend on voluntary contributions;

— the information is addressed to systems integrators, commercial and marketing people, venture capitalists, consultants and other researchers;

— the database is updated regularly to ensure accurate, relevant information.

For further information contact:

Longman Cartermill Ltd
Technology Centre
St Andrews
Fife, KY16 9EA
UK.

Telephone: 0334 77660 or +44 334 77660 or DG XIII's Help Line in Luxembourg: 010 352 45 30 30 or +352 45 30 30.

PREPARATION OF PROPOSALS

There is a great deal of competition for participation in Community programmes. The chance of gaining acceptance can be increased by careful presentation of the proposal. The basic ground rules are:

— organisations from more than one member state must be involved in the project;

— at least one partner must be an industrial company;

— the industrial partner must be prepared to contribute half of the costs that it will incur.

In addition, there are some issues that will attract 'brownie points' such as:

— the objectives of the project should relate to other general aims of the Community, eg aid to a developing region, contribution to improving the skilled workforce, aid to SMEs, improvement of the quality of life;

— there is a plan for carrying the result of the project through to marketable products;

— the participating organisations have a good record of achievement — it may be advisable to seek a partner who has already established a track record for successful participation in Community projects;

— the participants should be able to demonstrate full commitment to the project;

— the participants should be able to demonstrate that they can work together to achieve the objectives;

— the project must, of course, have well-defined objectives, a realistic budget, an efficient management structure and a clear programme for evaluation of its results.

This list is by no means exhaustive but it gives some idea of the factors taken into account by the Commission's assessors when trying to decide which of the many submissions they should put forward for support from the limited resources available.

5 Collaborative Programmes in Education and Training

INTRODUCTION

The skills shortage has been acknowledged throughout the Community as one of the most serious limitations to achieving full industrial potential. This applies even more to the informatics-related industries. The Community has addressed the problem by mounting a series of programmes aimed at improving collaboration throughout Europe in education and training in higher technology. Again, collaboration has been encouraged between higher educational institutions in different member states and between universities (a term often used in Europe to include institutions of further and higher education) and industrial companies.

The training and education programmes have other objectives in addition to the particular aims of addressing the skills shortage. The Community wishes also to:

— raise the level of achievement for all of its citizens;

— improve the capability for interchange of views between people in different member states — hence the language-related programmes;

— facilitate the mobility of workers, students and the population in general between different member states;

— encourage all people in the Community to look upon themselves as European in addition to, not instead of, their national affiliations.

87

This chapter outlines some of the programmes most applicable
to informatics. Organisations are urged to consider participation
in these programmes in order to improve the number and quality
of people available to work effectively in both supplier and user
companies, and in the education and training professions
themselves.

It may be noted that the programmes deal with both training
for the informatics profession and the use of informatics to
improve the quality of education and training in all areas — such
as in the DELTA programme.

EUROTECNET II

EUROTECNET II is an action programme (within the Framework
Programme) for vocational training and technological change. Its
predecessor, EUROTECNET I, ran from 1985-1988 and was aimed
at encouraging the interchange of information and experience
related to training in informatics.

The further development of training in this sector is seen by the
Community as important due to the pace of technological
development which leads to changes in professional roles,
creation of new qualification requirements and alterations in the
nature of industrial relationships. The completion of the single
market will also change the pattern of labour mobility and
increase the value of qualifications.

During EUROTECNET I, new technologies were used
increasingly for the training itself, making the training more
effective and economic, and also changing the function of the
trainers. EUROTECNET II will continue the basic structure of
having a series of demonstration projects but will be aimed
increasingly at building links between individual projects from
several member states. It is also being extended beyond the field
of informatics to cover the whole range of skills called for by the
development of new technologies.

The specific objectives of EUROTECNET II are:

—   to improve the capacity for basic and continuing training
     in the Community to take account of technological

changes and their impact on employment, work and qualifications;

— to assist in the design and development of future training provision, in order to take account of implications of future technological developments for new and existing occupations and to provide for the necessary new skills and qualifications required.

The first objective includes transnational co-operative ventures for exchanging expertise, particularly in certain areas, such as informatics, or in less well developed regions. A Community-wide clearing house for the exchange of learning materials has been set up.

The second objective will help in preparing plans for training provision, and projects on new training methods will be given priority. Links with other Community R&D programmes which have implications for training are being established.

The Community envisages two approaches for the achievement of these objectives:

— a set of principles to be used by member states for the development and improvement of training policies, and

— a series of future Community measures to support and supplement the actions taken within the member states.

What Member States are Expected to Achieve

Member States' operations under EUROTECNET II should:

— strengthen co-operation at all levels between the vocational training systems, including public and private sectors, employers and employees and all sections of the economy;

— raise the level of vocational training for the employed workforce, in respect of the impact of technological change, with particular regard to SMEs;

— stimulate innovation in experimental or demonstration training actions, with wide dissemination of information;

— enable unemployed young people to enter employment through the provision of training;

— promote equal opportunities for men and women, particularly by the retraining of women;

— promote the training and re-training of trainers in order to upgrade social and technical skills, including the use of multi-media methods.

What the Community will do

The following measures will reinforce the actions of Member States:

— promote the use of innovative approaches in adapting training to technological change, including the core activity — a Community-wide network of innovative demonstration projects;

— strengthen the links between Member States, including the encouragement of links between projects and the setting up of a clearing house for exchange of learning materials and the organisation of transnational study visits;

— improve the capacity of Member States to derive the greatest benefit from EUROTECNET II, including the setting up of a mechanism in each Member State for the dissemination of information on the impact of the programme; advice and consultancy services to Member States in order to identify training needs; a model scheme for the training of trainers; and a series of publications;

— provide for adaptation of future training systems, including research and analysis, with priority given to training for disadvantaged groups and developing training approaches which are designed to anticipate future needs and multiply the effects of investment in technology;

— arrange information activities, such as high-level demonstration conferences, training seminars, colloquia, workshops and round tables.

EUROTECNET II is proposed to extend over five years from the beginning of 1990 and its proposed budget from 1988-1992 is ECU 29 million; of which ECU 21.5 million is expected to come from the European Social Fund. The basic funding of the projects will be responsibility of the Member States, but projects considered eligible under the national programmes may qualify for extra funding from the European Social Fund.

For further information contact:

Technical Assistance Unit
EUROTECNET
66 Ave de Cortenbergh
1040-BRUSSELS
Belgium.

Telephone: 010 322 732 2000 or +322 732 2000.

COMETT

COMETT stands for *COMmunity action in Education and Training for Technology.* In COMETT the Community agreed to promote training programmes for students, engineers, technicians and managers. The range of technology and enterprise covered is wide, but the prime objective is to encourage training to ensure a fully competitive Europe. In order to achieve the more rapid assimilation of advanced research and development throughout the Community, the COMETT initiative provides funds to support training partnerships. These are trans-national and between universities/higher education establishments and enterprises. In addition, a particular concern of the initiative is to ensure that smaller and medium sized enterprises (SMEs) should benefit from the programmes thus developed.

Training, or rather retraining, is particularly important in areas of high technology where there is a need to ensure that appropriate skills are available and maintained. As an example, the University of London Industry Training Partnership is specifically interested in education and training in micro-electronics, the particular area being the branch of semi-conductor technology concerned with design of very large scale solid state circuits. The interest in forming the Partnership arose because of two investigations, one by the UK, the other by the Community, both of which reported large skill shortages in this subject.

COMETT STRUCTURE

In order to achieve its objectives the COMETT activity is provided with a small headquarters staff as administrators who act as a Technical Assistance Unit. Each member country also has an Information Centre. The operating structure was originally planned with five divisions, or 'Strands' as they are termed by COMETT. At present, these are as follows:

—   Strand A: This is the development strand under which University and Enterprise Training Partnerships (UETPs) are formed and run. The partnership must be between enterprises and universities/institutes of higher education.

—   Strand B: Under this category exchange placement programmes are organised. The exchanges must be between universities and enterprises or vice versa. A minimum period is also laid down, with 3 to 6 months typically encouraged.

—   Strand C: This strand is that under which short training programmes are developed. Inputs from enterprises are particularly encouraged; the programmes should apply across Europe, preferably with trans-national co-operation. Programmes for the training of trainers receive high priority.

—   Strand D: This strand was formed to encourage the development of multi-media training aids. Projects can be based on various information and communication technologies, with a strong emphasis on the European dimension.

— Strand E: This category was introduced for the activities which, though educational, did not fit comfortably within the previous Strands.

The initial COMETT phase is just being completed. The successor, COMETT II, has obtained preliminary agreement and is shortly expected to be agreed formally. Under COMETT II, Strands C and D will almost certainly be combined, and Strand E may be re-defined or abolished.

Partnerships in COMETT may be of two main types. The first is defined as a *Regional Partnership,* which is formed to provide for education/training requirements within a geographical area. It covers a broad field of technologies and aims to ensure that training courses are available to meet the existing and future demands of that area.

The second is termed a *Sectoral Partnership.* This type of partnership is one formed to produce material addressed to specific areas of technology, using a very wide definition of technology. Courses and material thus developed are available directly to industry and to Regional Partnerships. With both partnerships, trans-national interests are required. As an example, the University of London Industry Training Partnership is a sectoral UETP.

The number of UETPs of all classifications is over 1000.

The organisation of a UETP

The initial organising of a partnership is difficult to describe but one ingredient seems to be essential — an enthusiast who, by using existing contacts, may be able to build the foundation of a partnership. trans-national partners almost certainly will be obtained in this fashion. The contacts thus made may themselves be able to suggest further contacts. Once these initial contacts have been made successfully, suggestions for a proposal can be drawn up, and all prospective partners asked to send written confirmation of their willingness to take part in the new UETP. The enthusiast will probably have to take responsibility for the proposal. So far, many of those responsible for organising COMETT proposals have had an academic background.

All UETPs need to match COMETT funding. COMETT on Strands A, C, D and E provides partial support for any accepted programme. The balance can be provided in kind — manpower, office accommodation and/or money. In the case of Strand B (that involved with exchange placement programmes), a rather different arrangement is made whereby a grant is payable to those partaking, plus funding for administration, lecturer visits to students, etc.

Care has to be taken over funding in kind. There must be enough ready cash available for salaries, travel, printing and the other activities for which 'real' money is necessary. Running expenses can vary tremendously. With a large number of active participants, administrative expenses can be considerable. The trans-national involvement incurs increased travel and communication costs. The postal services across Europe cannot always be relied on for rapid communication, so that the use of fax or courier-type services is often required. Telephone charges are also significant.

It should be noted that all funding provided so far has been on a year-by-year basis. With COMETT I, an unexpectedly large number of good applications meant that the level of support per project had to be reduced from that originally proposed. For COMETT II some differences in the funding arrangements may be made, but preliminary warning has been given that support can be expected for three years only, possibly on a diminishing scale. The additional funding necessary for success in a project comes in many forms, but, in general, a combination of methods is used. After three years, all partnerships will probably be expected to be self-supporting.

Not unnaturally, there are considerable differences between partnerships. Many forms of organisation are acceptable to COMETT. Most seem to work! Partnerships vary from the very formal and legal approach to the very informal. Nearly all have a 'Co-ordinator', who may be employed full-time, part-time, or on fully-supported secondment.

In the formation period, a written commitment to join a partnership is necessary for inclusion in a COMETT submission; this can be difficult to obtain. Should a financial contribution also be requested, this can add to the difficulty of starting. Even once a contact is gained, it still takes time to become organised, to go beyond the formalities and to form the necessary good working relationships. Some trans-national partners within UETPs have found it difficult in practice to co-operate as they had planned because of funding restrictions. Others overcome the difficulties by allocating course development areas on a country-by-country basis. This may not be the most desirable way of working but it is understandable. Restricted opportunities to meet initially, for whatever reason, do seem to increase the time required to form effective working relationships. The time required to form the necessary good working relationships must be taken into consideration in any planning exercise.

A number of the UETPs which operate successfully are essentially based on pre-existing relationships. Many regional partnerships are strongly linked to activities, such as PICKUP in the UK, or to Chambers of Commerce in France. Words of warning have been heard about the size of UETPs, particularly those with 20 or more members; it has been suggested that smaller numbers, but more active membership, would be preferable. How one determines initially who will be active is difficult; doubtless most UETPs have received enthusiastic letters of interest for their COMETT proposals, but subsequently have heard nothing. And it should be remembered that a small number of partners does not necessarily ensure active participation by all.

The number of successful placements under Strand B is steadily increasing. The most successful are almost always those UETPs whose members have already had sandwich-type placement experience. Some interesting experiences of Visiting Fellowships have also been reported.

Strand C is seeing the development of various training courses. Some UETPs have utilised the strengths of groups of members to produce courses and some of these groups are on a country-by-country basis.

Publicity

Marketing and publicity are major problems; it would seem that few organisations have heard, or know, of COMETT. All UETPs are obliged to mention COMETT in their marketing material, but it seems that this is not particularly effective at publicising the COMETT programme. More widespread and vigorous marketing of the need for training and why COMETT was formed is necessary.

A strong marketing/publicity exercise will often be required at a project level. Probably many UETPs, and possibly COMETT itself, underestimated the magnitude of the task. Discovering the skills shortage is one thing, but persuading companies to take action is quite different. There is a need to educate enterprises of the requirement for continuous retraining and updating. Mail shots, advertising, etc, all cost money, hence the necessity to ensure that funds are available.

The future

COMETT is succeeding in many ways. As is inevitable with any development programme, there have been hiccups. The positive note is that COMETT is bringing together Community enterprises and educationalists in new ways. In addition to the contractual activity, there are benefits being gained which are also helping to bring forward a harmonised and competitive Europe. The Commission's DG XXIII, formed to assist SMEs, and COMETT are co-operating closely.

For anybody considering participation in a COMETT II activity, it is worth investigating whether a UETP already exists which has interests along the lines of those being considered. Most UETPs welcome additional active interest. As an example, ULITP would be very pleased to hear from anyone interested in the micro-electronic and related fields, and particularly from enterprises. The person to contact is:

> Mr A H Kent, COMETT Co-ordinator
> University of London Industry Training Partnership
> King's College, Strand, London WC2R 2LS, UK
>
> Telephone: 071 873 2773 or + 44 71 873 2773

The comment 'particularly from enterprises' is highly applicable. Surveys have shown that retraining is required over wide areas of technology. The complaint often raised is that courses are not relevant and do not consider the practical requirements of industry. COMETT is the opportunity to ensure practicality, but industry must participate if this is to be effective.

For more informatin please contact:

Technical Assistance Unit
COMETT
71 Ave de Cortenbergh
1040-BRUSSELS
Belgium.

Telephone: 010 322 733 9755 or +322 733 9755.

DELTA

DELTA (Developing European Learning through Technological Advance) is funded by the Commission as part of the Framework Programme. It is administered through DG XIII. The current exploratory phase of the DELTA Programme follows studies carried out between June and October 1986 and reported in July 1988 in the publication 'DELTA: Initial Studies'. Proposals were requested from consortia representing more than one Community Member State with an industrial partner and one organisation, either educational or from the training sector, representing the 'learning interest'. Thirty collaborative projects were funded. Projects will run for a total of 24 months from their starting date with a total budget of ECU 20 million.

The aim of the current phase is to investigate the application of new technology to learning, particularly open and distance learning, as a means of improving access to learning and meeting increased future learning needs through a Community-wide learning system.

The current programme is structured around five Action Lines:

Action Line 1: Learning Systems Research

The objective is to optimise the use of learning technologies across the Community. Mechanisms will be developed for the exchange and dissemination of information. Work in progress includes the setting up of a European Learning Technology Association (ELTA); organisation of annual DELTA conferences; a 'Who's Who' of European producers of learning technology materials; and an interactive newsletter on DELTA.

Action Line 2: Collaborative Development of Advanced Learning Technology

This is the largest area of work in the DELTA Programme and aims to contribute to the design of systems and equipment to support Community-wide open learning. The main thrust of the action is the development of a Portable Educational Tool Environment (PETE) to provide a uniform platform and software tools for the authoring and production of technology-based learning materials. Other work in progress in this line includes the specification of a learner workstation, expert system shells for learner modelling, specification of an intelligent tutoring and monitoring system and investigation of issues concerning the human computer interface.

Acton Line 3 : Testing and Validation of Communications and of SOFT (Satellite Open Testing Facility — for learning)

The aim of this action line is to take advantage of advances to the benefit of learning technology. Most of the projects in this action line are a test-bed for communications developments, exploring different contexts or addressing particular target groups. Work in progress includes learning applications for ISDN or terrestrial networks and satellites; distributed authoring and production of material and multi-lingual broadcasting.

Action Line 4: Interoperability

The action line addresses the standardisation requirements for European learning technology by identifying the required standards and incorporating or amending existing standards. Work in progress includes interfacing and protocols for telecommunications applications in education; recommendations on generally applicable user interfaces; and standards for authoring and learning environments.

Action Line 5: Promotion of Favourable Conditions

The aim is to determine the favourable conditions, including legal, market and economic factors, which affect take-up and usage of learning technologies. Work in progress concerns identification of barriers to the take-up of technology-based learning systems by SMEs, and case studies of good practice in open and distance learning.

In November 1989 a mid-term review of all current projects was carried out by the Commission supported by expert panels. The conclusion drawn from this review was that, in general, good progress was being made towards programme and project objectives. The programme had been particularly successful in identifying and bringing together the key factors in the learning technology field and initiating work on key developments for the future. The Commission is also developing plans for a further phase of DELTA which is commonly known as DELTA Main Phase.

Current suggestions for DELTA Main Phase propose a programme to follow the current Exploratory Action which would last 3-5 years.

The scope of the new programme would cover both R & D activities and exploitation of existing technologies, but on a European, rather than on a national or regional scale. The main lines of action suggested are:

— to prepare industry for the emerging common market in educational services and tools;

— to stimulate medium to long term investment in learning technology;

— to enable cost-effective learning to take place;

— to overcome regional problems in the Community and to cater for special learning needs;

— to prepare a basis for the promotion of European technology services and tools.

The Main Phase would also continue and extend work begun under the Exploratory Action. Three technical panels have been convened by the Commission comprising expert representatives from each Member State. Their task has been to draft a detailed plan for the Main Phase. While this has not formally been accepted or proposed by the Commission, the work of the technical panels has been carried out in the following three areas:

— Learning Technologies: hardware and software issues on workstations;

— Learning Technology Infrastructures: market, technical, regional and sectoral infrastructures for advanced learning technologies;

— Learning Technology Pedagogics; learning environments, learning modelling, assessments, cross language communication, interaction and the design environment.

The Commission expects to issue a call for proposals in March 1991, and submissions would then need to be in by June 1991.

Further information is available from Mike Rogers at the usual address for DG XIII; telephone: 010 322 236 3505 or + 322 236 3505.

ERASMUS

ERASMUS is the EuRopean community Action Scheme for the Mobility of University Students. It will be at least as important for students of informatics as for students of other subjects. There are four strands to the programme:

1. An extension and enlargement of the JSP (Joint Study Programme) scheme to provide a European University network of exchanges;

2.   Support of individual students who wish to take part in the exchange process;

3.   Specific action to improve academic recognition of qualifications. This includes a beefing-up of the NARIC (National Academic Recognition Information Centre) network activity;

4.   Various other measures to promote student mobility.

Mutual academic recognition is central to the whole ERASMUS process, which was approved by the Council in June 1987. The existing JSP and SSV (Short Study Visit) schemes have illustrated the way in which such schemes serve to accelerate the mutual recognition of qualifications. As a result, it is reasonable to expect that the ERASMUS programme, which will commit a budget of ECU 175 million over the three years 1987, 1988 and 1989 in what is seen as the first stage of a rolling programme, will improve the situation on the mutual recognition of qualifications in Europe. Since the problem of mutual academic recognition lies at the heart of the mutual recognition of professional qualifications and status in Europe, its solution of the problem is critical.

During the first two years, there have been 2909 applications aimed at improving inter-university collaboration; 80 per cent were for student mobility involving 23,000 students.

For further information contactr:

    Anna Badila
    Task Force for Human Resources — Education, Training
        and Use
    37 Rue Joseph II
    1040-BRUSSELS
    Belgium

    Telephone: 010 322 235 6514 or +44 322 235 6514.

LINGUA

The Community's LINGUA programme aims to encourage people to learn foreign languages in order to develop communication skills within the Community workforce. Within informatics, English is well established as the *lingua franca* mainly due to the leading role played by US companies' (who use a close approximation to English!). Nevertheless, it is important to produce manuals and other documentation in the native language of prospective users when trying to expand into markets where English is not the native tongue. Funding for LINGUA is expected to be about ECU 200 million over the five years from 1 January, 1990, although substantial expenditure will only begin in 1991.

There will be five lines of action:

—	grant support for in-service training of foreign-language teachers and trainers;

—	grant support for the development of inter-university co-operation programmes, allowing students to spend part of their course in the country whose language they are studying;

—	grant support for the development of language training in firms;

—	grant support for educational exchanges for young people in professional, vocational and technical education;

—	establishment of networks of communication and technical support.

A new LINGUA unit is now in place to administer, or assist the Commission in administering, these lines of action. Please contact:

> Annelize Keyman
> Task Force for Human Resources — Education, Training
>   and Use
> 3 Bureau 27
> 37 Rue Joseph II
> 1040-BRUSSELS, Belgium.

> Telephone: 010 322 235 5608 or + 44 322 235 5608.

EUROTRA

EUROTRA is a programme run by DG XIII to develop programs for computerised translation. A budget of ECU 10 million has been requested for the two years 1990-1992. The proposed topics are:

— System development, testing and research;

— Linguistics research;

— Lexical resources.

For further information contact:

Sergei Perschke
DG XIII
Commission of the European Communities
Bureau 004, Batiment Jean Monnet
Plateau du Kirchberg
2920-LUXEMBOURG.

Telephone: 010 352 4301 3423 or + 352 4301 3423.

OTHER PROGRAMMES

There are many other programmes aimed at improving education and training throughout the Community which are relevant to informatics as much as to any other industry or application. As examples I can cite PETRA (action programme for vocational training of young people and their preparation for adult and working life) which aims to support and supplement Member States' efforts to make it possible for young people to receive two years vocational training after they have completed their compulsory full-time education, if they so wish; and TEMPUS (Trans-European Mobility Scheme for University Students) which aims to arrange exchanges of students or staff between universities in Central and Eastern Europe and those of the Community. Those described in detail above will give an indication of the way the Community programs work, are well established and are the most widely known.

These programmes can be effective only if willing participants are prepared to support them by committing effort as well as resources. This applies particularly to industrial and commercial enterprises. After all, they are going to be the main beneficiaries in the long term.

6 Standards and Open Systems

INTRODL

Standards   ssential requirement in most
activities   ficant benefits to the user,
supplier a

For the

— giv   luct or service meets a stated
  spe   safety aspects, performance,
  etc)

— allo   o be undertaken;

— red   g costs;

— ena   tain products from multiple
  sou   conditions and reduce costs;

— pro\   sers can influence suppliers on
  pro(

For the su_r

— reduce development costs by stipulating a common
  requirement;

— provide an environment in which suppliers can be assured
  that their products will interface with a common service;

—   provide a basis by which vendors' products interwork.

And, for the *community at large*, standards:

—   assist in the creation of open international markets;

—   remove some artificial trading barriers;

—   reduce the ability of individual nations or companies to
    create market leads through the use of proprietary
    standards or the creation of cartels.

The Community has acknowledged that standards can play a
vital role in improving the competitiveness of European industry
generally. For the informatics industry, and for users of
informatics systems (which is a very wide community), the
ESPRIT programme has made the development of, and
conformance with, standards an integral part of all projects. In
the directives on public procurement also the Community has
insisted on conformance with standards.

Standards are clearly beneficial and receiving great
encouragement from the Community but decision-making in the
area of technical standards has been painfully slow. One reason
is that various national laws and provisions have often acted to
discourage firms from seeking orders in other Member States.
Countries have been slow to make concessions in an effort to
protect their indigenous industries.

Another reason is that informatics systems and practices are
changing rapidly and it is difficult, with the cumbersome
procedures for setting standards, to keep pace. Quite often, by
the time consensus has been reached on a given standard, other
factors need to be taken into account that make it redundant.

The high rate of technological change is further exacerbated by
the high level of technical complexity of informatics systems and
the requirement to interconnect a large number of components
from a multiplicity of suppliers. Each supplier is supportive of
standards if it enables users to purchase his equipment to connect
to another supplier's system that is already installed. On the
other hand, suppliers prefer to sell additional equipment for their

own installed base and are not anxious to support standards that permit another supplier to take part of their market.

The main differences, therefore, between informatics standards and those used in other areas are:

— rapid change in technology;

— complexity of computer hardware and software interfaces;

— a preponderance of de facto standards.

In addition, there is a significant problem in ensuring that products and services conform to standards. This difficulty has resulted in the need to create a new testing infrastructure based on the principles established for standards developed in the past.

INFORMATICS STANDARDS

The history of computing is relatively short but has numerous examples of de facto standards being created by the major computer equipment suppliers, sometimes to create market opportunities. Traditionally, users have not devoted significant resources to the articulation of their needs. As a result, most of the early examples of standards were based on supplier dominance and the size and amount of use of a product or technique. These situations were acceptable in cases where a limited amount of communication between computers was required.

In the past, standards were required mainly for input and output media and computer languages. The latter provide examples of some of the earlier work on standards development based on a committee and consensus approach.

Recent emphasis on informatics standards has been brought about by the recognition that information management and its automation is a key strategic issue for most organisations, if not all of them. There is increasing pressure from senior management to make their implementation and use more effective. Whereas it had been possible to run companies based on the use of one computer type which mainly handled administrative computing, many new applications of strategic importance have been developed which require information or data exchange between different departments within an organisation or between different organisations. This objective could only be met by more intelligent and innovative use and application of standards. Users have, therefore, begun to understand the strategic significance of standards and the influence they have on a user's ability to achieve business objectives.

Nevertheless, users have found it difficult to translate a requirement into a specification for products and services. Their life would be easier if they could use a list of 'descriptors' or standards which defined all forms of interface between one component and another, or between the component and the 'outside world'.

Some users and purchasers of informatics systems have realised that they need to direct standards activity, based on their own business strategies. In particular, users wish to influence the priorities that are given to individual items of standards development. A number of organisations have formed pressure groups to achieve this objective and have contributed to the definition of interfaces such as the UK's Government Open Systems Interconnection Profile (GOSIP), Manufacturing Automation Protocol (MAP) and Technical Office Protocol (TOP). These groups set out not only to influence suppliers and standards developers, but to determine protocols and sets or profiles of standards that were the most appropriate for their industry. This was a major change in the standards scene. Other groups have been formed to address other issues, particularly system software, but they are largely supplier-dominated.

The great majority of informatics standardisation work is international in nature. This is hardly surprising when the major supply companies are international and operate in many countries around the world, and when major users of informatics are themselves international companies which need to communicate universally, and which need to have compatible information systems in the various countries in which they operate. The use of national standards in this field is now minimal, and all are agreed that international standards take precedence.

The four principal international standardisation bodies relevant to IT are CCITT (Telecommunications), CCIR (Radio Communications), IEC (Electrotechnical Standardisation) and ISO (General Standardisation). The last two have recently set up a Joint Technical Committee, called JTC1, to deal specifically with their overlapping interests in informatics work. This is now the principal body at an international level dealing with information systems standardisation, and its formation is of far-reaching importance which may well show the shape of the future.

At the European level the two European bodies which are equivalent to ISO and IEC, are CEN (European Committee for Standardisation) or CENELEC (European Committee for Electrotechnical Standards). As with the international bodies, these two have joined together to form an Information Technology Steering Committee to help plan the European work programme, and to have responsibility for the creation of European standards (EN).

It is the policy of the Community to adopt international standards whenever possible. Only where standards are needed, but are not available internationally within the limited timescale, is there the intent and motivation to create European standards. The Commission is prepared to provide both the resources and political pressure to impel such standards work to be undertaken.

EUROPEAN DIRECTIVES

The process of creating good standards requires a genuine effort to ensure that those who are interested parties (and therefore potential users of the standards) are satisfied with what is being produced. The process of reaching this agreement with industry at large is called 'consensus' and, if it is rushed and insufficient acceptance has been gained, the resulting standard will not be effective. To balance against this, however, we have the problem described above of rapidly changing technology. Some kind of compromise has to be found, and the Community's approach is such a compromise. The European standardisation programme is aligned to sets of directives whereby the public sector organisations within the Community are required to make use of the relevant standards in procurement processes. These directives are already in effect so far as OSI (Open Systems Interconnection) standards are concerned, and this has created pressures on the supply industry to develop products aligned to these standards.

Some effective measures introduced by the Community to ensure conformance with standards are as follows. First, under a procedure which has been in force since 1983, Member States are required to notify the Commission in advance of proposals for new technical regulations. This gives the Commission and other member states the chance to intervene if they judge that the regulation would create a new barrier to trade. These arrangements are proving an effective weapon in heading off new national barriers.

Secondly, under the Community's new approach to technical harmonisation agreed in 1985, the directive that create new Community-wide standards no longer need to specify a mass of technical detail. They are limited to setting the essential requirements for health, safety, consumer protection and the environment, with the technical details being worked out subsequently by CEN or CENELEC. All products which comply with these requirements will be allowed to circulate freely within the Community and no member state will be able to refuse them entry on technical grounds.

Of the directives already agreed under the 'new approach', the electro-magnetic compatibility directive is one that will have a direct effect on suppliers of informatics and telecommunications systems, since it applies to almost all electrical and electronic appliances, equipment and apparatus. The 'essential requirements' relate to non-generation of electro-magnetic disturbance and to immunity from such disturbance.

Compliance with these requirements will have to be demonstrated, which means testing and certification. National requirements for products to be re-tested and re-certified to gain entry to other countries' markets can act as a real barrier to trade.

That is why the Community is sponsoring the creation of a pan-European conformance testing programme to provide mechanisms to establish that products conform to standards, and to seek to encourage the mutual recognition of test results and certificates — to ensure that any product, which can be sold in the Member State in which it is produced, will be freely marketable in all other parts of the Community; unimpeded by different national standards, testing and certification practices.

Thirdly, two Acts (Council Decision 87/95 and Council Directive 88/295) require Member States to advertise public procurements, and to refer to appropriate standards, for procurements above ECU 100,000. They also require specific open purchasing procedures to be followed. This includes a mandatory requirement to specify the use of appropriate standards in these purchases. In informatics, any standard that has reached an appropriate level of maturity such as national, European or international status, must, therefore, be quoted in public procurement.

This legislation covers central and local government, including police, health and education authorities. Similar legislation is likely to affect purchases made by public utilities, some of which are in the private sector in the United Kingdom.

Whilst there are a number of derogations which enable public purchasers to escape the legislation, such as the need for compatibility, or the unavailability of appropriate standards, or the fact that the project is novel or innovative, most European public procurements will fall within these Acts. The combination of the Member States' public purchases is equivalent to tens of billions of ECU and ensures that suppliers pay proper attention to the market and its desire to use standards.

These directives have been welcomed by governments and the public sector in general. In public sector procurements and, indeed in all procurements, there is a proper requirement to obtain the best value for money from the purchase of products and services. The main method of meeting that objective is through competitive purchase. As a result of the implementation of this policy, there is an inevitable situation where different systems from multiple vendors are purchased which need to interwork. Experience has revealed that numerous problems emerge in a multi-vendor environment. The use of standards provides a solution to many of those problems. As a result central and local government bodies have given whole-hearted support to standards initiatives. European legislation has given additional impetus to the level of this support.

In addition to the legislation which has already had a significant effect on public procurement, the Commission has ensured that the standards development infrastructure in Europe has received appropriate attention and is being created to cover all issues. From the research projects, such as EUREKA, ESPRIT and RACE, to the standards development committees, such as European Workshop for Open Systems (EWOS), and to the conformance test authorities, Europe is playing an active role.

ACCREDITATION AND CERTIFICATION

In the past, the process of testing, accreditation and certification was managed essentially on a country-by-country basis. The Commission's endorsement of OSI as a mechanism for opening up the informatics market has been translated into CEN's programme for defining European norms.

The next logical step was to address the problem of testing, certification and accreditation. A programme was set up by the Commission in 1985 to harmonise Conformance Testing Services (CTS), which resulted in a methodology to harmonise the testing of OSI products and the services offered by test laboratories throughout Europe.

The entire European scheme of providing a technical basis for a pan-European scheme to ensure equivalence of results and mutual recognition of certificates between Member States was adopted in March 1986 by the ITSC (Information Technology Steering Committee).

The ECITC (European Committee for Information Technology Certification) — comprising representatives from national organisations throughout the Community and EFTA — was set up to implement this scheme under which various Recognition Arrangements (RAs), which report directly to ECITC, are responsible for co-ordinating activity in specific functional testing areas. Two such RAs are currently being set up: OSTC (Open Systems Testing Corporation — wide area network applications) and ETCOM (European Testing for Conformance for Office and Manufacturing Committee — local area network applications).

OPEN SYSTEMS

Every person and organisation appears to have a different definition of Open Systems. The term can be broadly defined as 'Open Systems use standards to enable information handling products and services purchased from multiple suppliers to operate together effectively'. Open Systems include the operating system, database, communications, data and information interchange, user interface, system and program development, management and security. Each of these areas already has a number of associated *de jure* and sometimes *de facto* standards, but there is no overall framework or architecture to describe how the standards themselves in those areas interwork. Individual suppliers have made considerable progress in this area since, in general, their task is made easier by the limited nature of their own standards. In Open Systems, however, all areas and views need to be taken into account, leading to the emergence of a potentially complex picture.

Many organisations claim to be working on a framework for Open Systems, but the process is difficult and the output is probably a multi-dimensional model. This would not necessarily help the thrust for simplicity. An important aspect, therefore, is the decomposition of an informatics system into commonly agreed elements since the smaller functional units are easier to manage and easier to specify. The specifications need to be precise, so that purchasers know exactly what they are getting when they ask a supplier to provide a particular component. Furthermore, there needs to be industry-wide acceptance of what each component does.

The goals of precise definition and consensus are achieved through international consultation. The main organisations involved are ISO (The International Standards Organisation) and CCITT (The international body of telephone and telegraphy administrations).

Open Systems model

Many methods of decomposition are possible. Figure 6.1 presents the model used by CCTA (Central Computer and Telecommunications Agency), the department of the UK's Treasury that provides advice to UK Government departments on their informatics strategies. Their model reflects the international consensus on Open Systems components.

In general, the components at the top of the diagram are closest to the user's applications whilst those further down provide supporting services. The underlying computer hardware and communications cabling (physical environment) are at the bottom of the diagram. The key to the success of the approach is agreeing on how each component relates to the outside world. When each element has a known functionality and a well-defined interface, purchasers can specify what they want without being concerned about how it is achieved. Furthermore, this modular approach allows different parts of a total system to be bought from different suppliers. This means that vendors must compete on price, quality and support rather than relying on binding customers into a single set of products.

Users will only be concerned with what happens right at the top of the diagram — the actual business applications that their computers are supporting. These applications may be implemented using packages, particularly for common systems like payroll or accounts. Others might be bespoke developments — although these will benefit from using a standard set of tools such as PCTE, the Portable Common Tools Environment developed as an ESPRIT project. PCTE helps in two ways. First, applications can be consistent with each other because they use the same underlying mechanisms for screen handling, data access and information presentation. Secondly, applications can be moved from one system supporting PCTE to another with minimal difficulty.

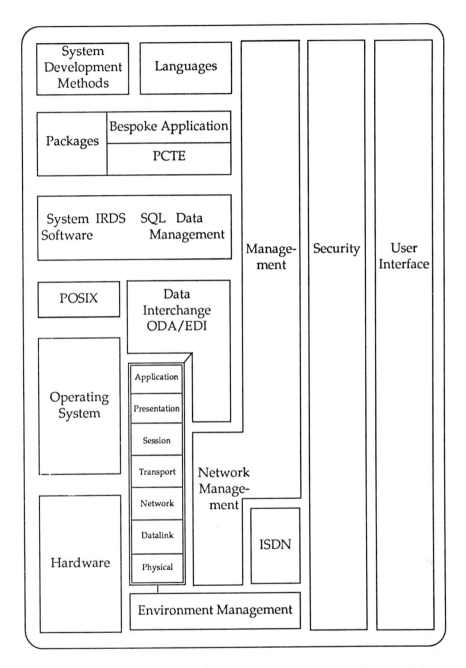

Figure 6.1: Open Systems Environment — the model used by the Central Computing and Telecommunications Agency (CCTA) which is responsible for advising all UK government departments on their informatics strategies

Both packages and bespoke applications should use a common set of data management facilities. The CCTA diagram shows SQL, the Structured Query Language, and IRDS the Information Resource Dictionary System. If applications are built on top of these then the management of information can be kept entirely separate from the programs that create, modify and retrieve that information.

To the right of the diagram are three pillars that represent functions that are common throughout an informatics system — user interface, security and management — which need to be applied to business applications and right down through to the lowest nuts and bolts of the physical components.

A functional split occurs below the data management box, with POSIX on the left and data interchange on the right. This reflects the distinction between what goes on inside a computer system and what goes on between computer systems. Positioning data management above this split allows information to be considered independently of its location in a distributed network.

POSIX standards have been derived from the UNIX (a proprietary trademark of AT&T) interface but differ in a number of ways — partly so that no individual supplier's implementation of UNIX will have a head start. POSIX does not attempt to define an operating system, merely a standard interface. An example of how this will be implemented is provided by Digital, who have announced that their proprietary (and non-UNIX) operating system VAX/VMS will be enhanced with a standard POSIX interface to system services. Other leading vendors, including IBM, have announced support for POSIX. Software developers will cease to target their products at particular hardware and will instead aim to run them on a standard POSIX platform.

On the right of POSIX, the diagram shows data interchange support. Standards in this area are concerned with the structure of information and the two most important are shown. ODA, the Office Document Architecture, provides an agreed format for word processing and desktop publishing files. It allows documents created on one office system to be transferred to another whilst retaining formatting codes, font descriptions, graphics and features such as paragraph numbering. Leading suppliers supporting ODA include ICL, Bull and Siemens.

Electronic Data Interchange (EDI), as described in Chapter 3, has emerged as an important enabler for better business communications. Early proprietary and *de facto* standards are being replaced by the internationally agreed EDIFACT message formats.

Electronic Data Interchange is supported by the original set of OS standards — OSI (Open Systems Interconnection) — commonly represented as a seven layer model. Since this area has been more extensively developed than any other, I can give a fuller description.

THE OSI REFERENCE MODEL

The International Standards Organisation (ISO) set up a sub-committee (SC 16) in 1977 to develop OSI. The OSI Basic Reference Model was approved as ISO 7498 in 1984 and there have been a number of enhancements and extensions since. Many of the other important standards have recently reached the final International Standard (IS) level, but others are still in the early stages of the standardisation process.

The Reference Model (RM) is an abstract model used to provide a framework to describe the open systems aspects of communications between computer systems. It does not describe the actual behaviour of real systems nor how the services and protocols that it describes are actually implemented.

The first assumption of the RM is that the open systems communicate through physical media. At present only telecommunications media have been considered, though other interconnection media are not excluded.

The second important feature of the RM is the concept of layering. This is so fundamental to the philosophy of the RM that it is frequently referred to as the "Seven Layer Model" (Figure 6.2). The seven layers are Application, Presentation, Session,

Transport, Network, Data Link and Physical. The purpose of the layering is to separate out the various different functions required to provide communications services.

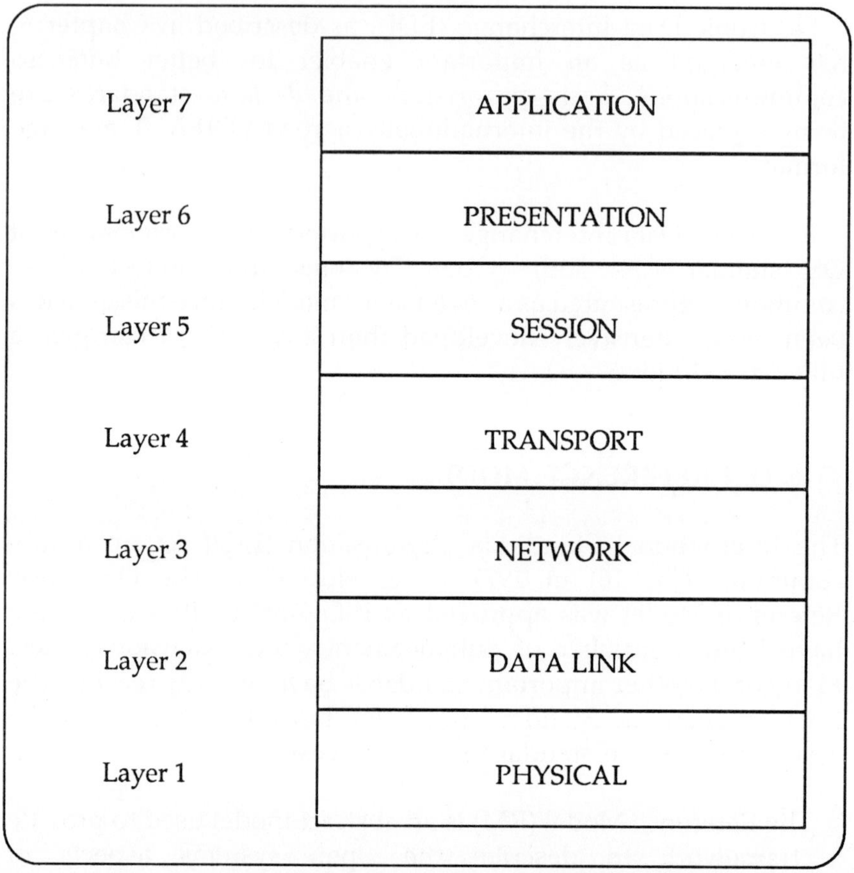

Layer 7	APPLICATION
Layer 6	PRESENTATION
Layer 5	SESSION
Layer 4	TRANSPORT
Layer 3	NETWORK
Layer 2	DATA LINK
Layer 1	PHYSICAL

Figure 6.2: The Seven Layer Model

The operation of each layer can be designed separately and only needs to know how to interface with the layers immediately above and below it. Each layer uses services provided by the layer below and provides services to the layer above, using a defined interface through service access points.

The implementation of a layer of the model, known as a 'layer entity' in OSI terminology, communicates with the peer entities in the same layer in remote open systems, using a defined protocol by means of the layers beneath it and the underlying physical medium (Figure 6.3).

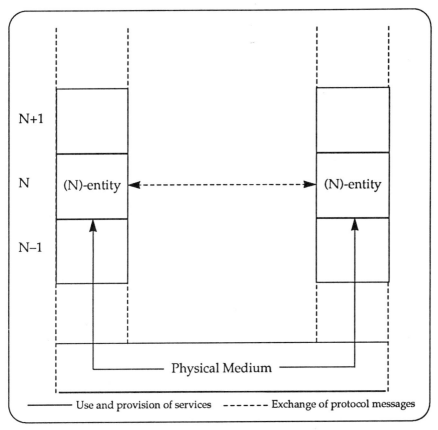

Figure 6.3: Communication between Peer Entities

The Seven Layers

The *application* layer provides a means by which the application process gains access to the OSI environment. It provides both services specific to particular applications, such as file transfer, and common service functions used by a number of applications. Note that the user interface is above this layer and is not covered by the OSI RM. Sometimes the user is referred to as Layer 8.

The *presentation* layer deals with the management of data for the application entities. It provides a common language or syntax for the two end systems to communicate. It can provide translations between different machine character codes like ASCII and EBCDIC and, only theoretically at the moment, translation between different languages such as English and French.

Encryption and data compression can also be provided.

The *session* layer provides mechanisms to establish, organise and synchronise the dialogue between the end systems and to manage their data exchange. One feature of this layer is checkpointing. This allows recovery from a network failure during a session without having to start all over again.

The *transport* layer provides the transparent transfer of data between end systems and can optimise the use of the underlying network layer. It provides end to end delivery, multiplexing, splitting and error detection and recovery.

The *network* layer provides a means to establish, maintain and terminate network connections between end systems. It provides flow control, switching and routing across sub-networks.

The *data* layer is concerned with passing data between nodes of the sub-network, not necessarily end systems. It delivers data over a single link and can also provide error detection.

The *physical* layer is concerned with the physical aspects of the communications to actually provide the transmission of bits of data.

As originally defined the OSI RM describes only connection-oriented communication. A connection at any particular layer is established, used and then closed down. This is not appropriate to some applications, such as transaction processing, and an addendum has been issued to the RM to cover connectionless communication. A major problem yet to be resolved is the practical interworking of connectionless and connection-oriented networks.

OTHER OSI STANDARDS

In addition to the Reference Model itself, OSI is made up of a large number of other standards, which may be split into three groups.

The first group describes the details of the services and protocols for each of the seven layers. They describe in detail how each layer uses services provided by the layer below and provides services to the layer above, and the protocols used between peer entities.

In the RM, the boundary between the network and transport layers has particular importance. In the transport layer and above, all protocol exchange is between end systems. In the network layer and below, communication may be with intermediate systems that are part of the networking infrastructure.

The second group of standards describes how different technologies and physical connections can be used to provide the OSI network service. For example, the standard ISO 8802 specifies the local area network (LAN) technologies. ISO 8802-3 is Carrier Sense Multiple Access with Collision Detection (CSMA/CD), commonly known as Ethernet, and ISO 8802-5 is the Token Ring technology. ISO 8878 specifies how X.25 can provide the COnnection mode Network Service (CONS). The number of OSI standards for different technologies is growing rapidly and this appears in some ways to be defeating one of the purposes of standardisation. One of the most recent technologies to enter the OSI lower layers standardisation process is the Fibre Distributed Data Interface (FDDI) which is a high bandwidth (100 Megabits per second) dual fibre optic ring technology.

A final group of standards describes the protocols for OSI applications that can provide services to users and it is this group that is most visible to those outside the specialised world of OSI experts. Many of these standards are already agreed or in the final stages of the standardisation process. ISO 8505 is MOTIS (Message-Oriented Text Interchange Systems) — 'electronic mail' in simpler language. This standard is technically aligned with the CCITT standard X.400 and will probably be the first widely used OSI application. Currently the wide range of different ways of sending international electronic messages creates a huge barrier to the effective use of the medium. MOTIS (also known as Message Handling Systems (MHS) by CCITT) is expected to resolve this problem. ISO 8751 is File Transfer Access and Management which will allow systems to transfer files between each other, access each others' files and perform other filestore operations remotely. Other standards cover areas such as Job

Transfer and Manipulation (ISO 8831), Virtual Terminals (ISO 9040) and Directories (ISO 9594).

Work has started in ISO on developing standards for security and management, but full standards in these areas are a long way off.

Many of the standards have a number of options within them for a variety of reasons, one being the different technologies that are available, another the functionality required from an application may vary from one real system to another. For example, the implementation of mail on a small personal computer may need to be much less sophisticated than on a large timesharing system. Some options are available merely because some of the member bodies could not agree on a single choice. In order to reduce these choices and to make interworking more likely a number of functional standards are being defined. In Europe, the functional standards produced by CEN and CENELEC are called European Norms (EN). For example the functional standard T/611 specifies how CSMA/CD LANs can provide the connection mode network service. Similar bodies elsewhere in the world are the National Bureau of Standards (NBS) in the USA and POSI in Japan.

IMPLEMENTATION OF OPEN SYSTEMS

Organisations should not expect to adopt Open Systems overnight. The important step is to introduce a procurement strategy that shows active preference in favour of standards. Planners need to analyse the computer systems in use today, those that will be required in future and where the necessary standards can be incorporated. Implementation of the strategy depends on product availability, but also on the right time for replacement of existing equipment when its useful life is over.

Migration to Open Systems requires careful planning and a good idea of achievable targets over the next five years. In the interim, each step should be justified in its own right and should be expected to provide tangible benefits along the way.

COSINE

Within the framework of EUREKA there is a unique project called COSINE (Co-operation on OSI Networking in Europe) which involves all the EUREKA countries as well as the Commission of the European Communities and Yugoslavia. Its objective is to provide networking support across Europe for all researchers in industry, universities and public laboratories.

The first service was introduced in March 1990, following the signing of a contract by the Commission on behalf of COSINE and PTT Telecom (Netherlands) for a pan-European backbone service which provides data networking interconnection between national research networks. Operating in accordance with the international X.25 standard, the IXI (International X.25 Interconnection) service will enable others, such as electronic mail, bulk data transfer and intercontinental gateways to be provided to researchers across Europe by interconnecting national research networks together. IXI is a pilot service which will explore the problems and possibilities and should lead to a more substantial and continuing service.

COSINE is intended to be a catalyst only; the long-term intention is to create an electronic infrastructure without the need for a continuing project. The basis of this must be individual, but closely co-ordinated, national actions; national plans (for research networking) are therefore being developed to assist each participating country to achieve the long-term objectives. Another prerequisite of success for a self-sustaining mechanism is that users must want, and be prepared to pay for, the services. This involves a difficult transition from the present arrangements in most countries with academic networks where the users do not, themselves, meet the cost of data networking.

IXI will be fully funded by COSINE for the first year while the many problems are investigated and appropriate levels of service are established. Beyond that time, however, charges will be introduced with the intention that the full costs of international connection are met by users by the end of the 3-year project.

COSINE is steered by a Policy Group with representatives from each participating country. This group is responsible for the allocation of funds within a total budget for the 3-year project of ECU 15 million for the 'core' projects to which all participants subscribe. A further ECU 20 million is budgeted for optional projects. The national financial contributions are made by the appropriate government departments. The Commission provides the secretariat for COSINE and also the project monitoring officer.

The chosen mechanism for COSINE is to call for proposals in connection with the development and supply of appropriate services. In some cases, it is possible to launch services immediately even if only on a pilot basis. In others, development or investigation is required and suitable projects must be launched first. In all cases, competitive bids are sought through the Calls for Proposals.

The publication of the Calls for Proposals, the selection and monitoring of the subsequent contracts and the overall management of the project are the responsibility of a COSINE Programme Management Unit (CPMU) now being established by RARE (Réseaux Associés pour la Récherche Européenne) described below. RARE operates the CPMU under contract from COSINE and has issued the first Call for Proposals dealing with directory and information systems. Further calls expected at the time of writing will be for gateway services to interconnect older, non-OSI systems into the network and for security (confidentiality) systems.

COSINE is using OSI products and addressing the related administrative, operational and even regulatory issues which are necessary to permit ready communication between a multiplicity of computer-based systems.

For the projects to achieve their objectives, it is essential to involve a wide range of users, suppliers and service operators. A COSINE Register has been established of organisations that wish to be informed of activities, with a view to participating. All interested organisations should contact either RARE or the COSINE Secretariat at the addresses listed below as soon as possible, indicating their particular interests if they wish to be placed on this register:

COSINE Secretariat
Commission of the European Communities
DG XIII A-2
Rue de la Loi 200
B-1049 BRUSSELS
Belgium.

Telephone: 010 322 235 5976 or + 322 235 5967.

RARE

RARE, an acronym for Réseaux Associés pour la Récherche Européenne, is the association of European reseach networking organisations and their users. Its aim is to foster co-operation between these organisations in order to develop a harmonised communications infrastructure and so enable researchers to communicate, to use information and to access computer resources throughout Europe and other continents.

In most European countries a computer communications (or networking) service for the research community has been introduced, such as the Joint Academic Network (JANET) in the UK, SURFNET in the Netherlands and DFN in Germany. These services are based on a variety of technologies, depending on national circumstances. As a result, communications with other groups, both nationally and internationally, can be difficult. In almost every European country programmes exist to harmonise networking facilities on a national scale, but there is a growing requirement amongst European researchers for international communications, based on the use of public telecommunications facilities, where these are suitable.

It is the objective of RARE to promote and participate in the establishment of a harmonised communications infrastructure for the research community based on OSI. The establishment of this infrastructure will provide an international complement to the national networking activities. In this work RARE fully supports the activities within EWOS (the European Workshop for Open Systems).

RARE has established a number of Working Groups which develop the detailed requirements for harmonised interworking. The groups hold regular meetings with the discussion continuing between meetings using distributed electronic mail and computer conferencing. These meetings are open to RARE members with additional outside experts invited as necessary.

Other activities of RARE include the annual Networkshop, to which attendees are invited via the representatives of the RARE members, thus ensuring a high technical level of discussion. And, of course, RARE is currently involved in COSINE and a number of other major projects.

Those wishing to obtain more information about RARE, including details of membership, copies of the Annual Report and reports on projects should contact:

> RARE Secretariat
> PO Box 41882
> Kruislaan 409
> Watergraafsmeer
> NL-1009 DB, AMSTERDAM
> The Netherlands.
>
> Telephone: 010 31 20 592 5078 or + 31 20 592 5078.
> E-mail raresec@nikhef.n1

SPAG

The Standards Promotion and Application Group (SPAG) was founded in 1983 as a 'round table' of European informatics companies. The Commission was also instrumental in the creation of SPAG to co-ordinate activities within Europe towards the development of European functional standards. SPAG became a company registered under Belgian law in 1986. SPAG's mission is to achieve an open international market for the computer and telecommunications industry, based on harmonised standards, and testing and certification of OSI products.

SPAG is involved actively in a wide range of Community research and other projects. In pursuing its mission SPAG:

— plays a leading role in the European Workshop on Open Systems (EWOS);

— influences the development of International Standards Profiles (ISPs) through the Feeders Forum;

— helps to shape the international harmonisation effort in conformance testing and certification;

— has recently been appointed to chair ETSI's Technical Committee for Advanced Test Methodology (SC2);

— collaborates with COS and the OS/Network Management Forum in the US to accelerate the availability and use of OSI standards and test technology for network management;

— publishes the Guide to Use of Standards (GUS) which represents the consensus opinion and support of SPAG's shareholders to developing current and future OSI functional standards and OSI conformance and IOP (Interoperability) testing methodology.

For further information please contact;

SPAG S.A.,
149, Ave. Louise
Box 7
1050-BRUSSELS
Belgium.

Telephone: 010 322 535 0840 or + 322 535 0840.

EFFECT ON EUROPEAN INDUSTRY

Clearly, informatics standards are going to become increasingly important to industry, and the openness of markets addressed by industry will depend upon their reaction to the demands of the standardisation process. Industries, whether they be informatics suppliers or informatics users, will have to make sure that they are aware of the developing standards process and its application to their particular interests. Users, in particular, will increasingly want to influence the standardisation programme, to apply pressure and, if necessary, resources to getting what they want. There is already a significant change in the way the standardisation processes work in Europe; in 1988 two new organisations were formed which show this. These were, first, the European workshop for Open Systems (EWOS) which has taken over from the European standardisation bodies (CEN/CENELEC) with the task of developing European functional standards, that is standards appropriate to the application of information technology in a user environment. This body works in parallel with similar bodies in the United States and Japan and cooperates with them and JTC1, making sure that European interests are protected in the wider international development scene. The second new body is the European Telecommunications Standards Institute (ETSI) which, as its name implies, has been set up as a formal European standardisation body in the area of telecommunications. With the convergence of communications and information technologies, the Community will want to ensure that there is close liaison between this body and informatics standards bodies.

OTHER ADDRESSES

The address for CEN, CENELEC and CEPT (the Conference of European Postal and Telecommunications administrations) is:

> 2 Rue Brederode
> Bte 5,B, 1000-BRUSSELS, Belgium.
>
> Telephone: 010 322 519 6811 or + 322 519 6811.

The section of the British Standards Institution (BSI) dealing with informatics standards is at:

> 205 Holland Park Avenue
> LONDON, W11 4XB.
>
> Telephone: 071 629 9000 or + 44 71 629 9000.

7 Legislation

INTRODUCTION

The previous chapters have described some of the regulations introduced by the Community to improve the competitiveness of the European informatics industry, and of industry generally, by, for example, requiring conformance with Open Systems in public procurements. This chapter addresses the Community's efforts to introduce common legislation related to informatics with social objectives, particularly the prevention of computer crime.

Most of this chapter is based on a report produced by the Committee on Crime Problems of the Council of Europe (see Chapter 1). The report addressed three aspects of computer related crime:

— the forms of crime (fraud, espionage, sabotage and misuse);

— the extent to which national law should be adapted;

— the extent to which European conventions apply or should be adapted.

Following consideration of that report, the Council recommended to its members that they take into account the recommendations, and produce guidelines for national legislatures when reviewing their legislation or initiating new legislation on computer-related crime.

The recommendation R(89)9 recognises "the importance of an adequate and quick response to the new challenge of computer-related crime" and, since this crime "often has a transfrontier character", there is a "resulting need for further harmonisation of the law and practice and of improving international legal co-operation".

It asks members to report to the Secretary General of the Council during 1993 of any developments in their legislation, judicial practice and experiences of international legal co-operation in respect of computer-related crime.

The report does not define computer-related crime, but instead lists specific offences. Certain types of computer-related crime have been excluded, eg trading in passwords.

One of the most effective means of preventing computer-related crime is the development and introduction of security measures, an approach which, when combined with efforts to increase awareness of the possibilities of abuse, is also regarded, even by criminal law experts, as being fundamentally more important and holding out greater prospects of success than enhanced criminal law protection. A concern for cost-effectiveness, however, will limit the security measures taken. The more secure a system is, the more difficult it is for legitimate users to do their work and the slower is the speed for doing any particular task. Thus, there is an indirect cost of security measures in addition to the costs of the security equipment and software.

A basic principle that the report adheres to is that every effort should be made to apply current law to new forms of crime as much as possible. In the actual practice of prosecution, this has also largely been the rule up to now.

There is now a new minimum list of computer crimes which represents "the special danger and harmfulness of a hard core of certain computer-related abuses that should be dealt with by the criminal law". These are fraud, forgery, damage, sabotage, and unauthorised access, interception and reproduction.

The Council recommends that those responsible for the development of national criminal policy and its conversion into legal provisions should allow themselves to be guided by this European consensus. Similar laws in member countries will facilitate international co-operation and will prevent abuses from being shifted to those states where the criminal law had previously been more lax.

The abuses put on the optional list, meaning that they should be given consideration where legislation is planned, are those where there was less of a consensus.

The procedural processes for law on computer crime (eg how to collect and use evidence in computer environments), have been relatively neglected. There are three main concerns:

—   the coercive powers of law enforcement authorities to gather evidence;

—   the specific legal problems of gathering, storing and linking personal data in criminal proceedings;

—   the admissibility of evidence consisting of computer records in criminal court proceedings.

These concerns have implications for international co-operation. Today it is technically possible to manipulate a keyboard in country A, thereby altering data stocked in country B, which is then transferred to country C and there obtain a fraudulent result, (eg payment). It is not clear which country should have jurisdiction to investigate and to prosecute. There are also difficulties in avoiding the creation of 'computer-crime havens'. The international harmonisation of the legal approach to computer-related crime should go some way to resolving these problems.

COMPUTER FRAUD

The report defines computer fraud as:

"The input, alteration, erasure or suppression of computer data or computer programmes, or other interference with the course of data processing, that influences the result of data processing thereby causing economic or possessory loss of property of another person with the intent of procuring an unlawful economic gain for himself or for another person or, alternatively, with the intent to unlawfully deprive that person of his property."

The registered number of cases in this category is not high except in the area of misuse of automatic cash dispensers. However, attacks against another's property by means of a computer usually cause remarkably high damage, says the report. Those attacks detected were mostly committed by insiders, often facilitated by the lack of sufficient control. The new crimes were mainly the result of input manipulations and, to a lesser extent, program manipulations.

COMPUTER FORGERY

This is defined as:

"The input, alteration, erasure or suppression of computer data or computer programmes, or other interferences with the course of data processing, in a manner or under such conditions, as prescribed by national law, that it would constitute the offence of forgery if it had been committed with respect to a traditional object of such an offence."

Forgery is normally preparation for fraud. The report wants falsification of data to be put on the same footing as the forgery of documents or other instruments. In some countries existing provisions on forgery of documents cover computer forgery. In England forgery provisions have been extended, in Australia they have been amended and in West Germany amendments have been made and a new offence of falsification of data with 'evidentiary value' has been created as well.

DAMAGE TO COMPUTER DATA OR COMPUTER PROGRAMS

The report identified "The erasure, damaging, deterioration or suppression of computer data or computer programs without right" as a crime.

In most of these cases the purpose is only to do harm. A common motive is revenge by an employee whose contract is being terminated. Other motives are political/ideological, as in terrorist acts and attempts to attract public attention, in many countries, new provisions or amendments to existing provisions have been made or proposed.

A more serious aspect of this crime is computer sabotage:

> "The input, alteration, erasure or suppression of computer data or computer programs, or interference with computer systems, with the intent to hinder the functioning of a computer or a telecommunications system. Hindering of the functioning of important public computer systems such as military, medical or traffic control computers, or private computers (bank or insurance company computers, for example) may not only have great economic consequences but may also lead to disastrous human consequences, even loss of life."

Preventive measures should play the most important role, but it is necessary for these to be supplemented by criminal law provisions. Several member states have already enacted or made criminal law proposals on this subject. The proposed legislative text does not impose any limits on the size of the system protected — it could be as small as a minicalculator — but countries may wish to do so.

UNAUTHORISED ACCESS

The report deals only with "The access without right to a computer system or network by infringing security measures." Since most systems have some security measures, such as passwords for authorised users, it is probably sufficient to limit the legislation to secure systems.

There are three aspects of unauthorised entry — where no damage is done and no further crime is committed, where damage is done to the system by altering data or programs, and where access is the means of using information to commit a further crime without necessarily changing the data or programs in the system.

Many students and enthusiasts, the so-called 'hackers', regard the existence of a computer system as a challenge to their ability to gain entry. Sometimes they leave messages to prove that they have succeeded. They defend their actions by claiming that they are helping the owner of the system to detect loop-holes in the security arrangements.

Some countries have legislation that can be used to punish behaviour which consists purely in gaining unauthorised access to a computer network (the Computer Misuse Bill in the UK, for example). The Community should give consideration to criminal law prevention of mere unauthorised access irrespective of whether security devices are overcome, and whether or not there is intention to commit a further crime.

In the first place, owners of data need to assure their data subjects that the system is secure and that no electronic 'peeping Tom' is able to invade their privacy. Thus, enormous expense has to be incurred to prevent sophisticated hackers from gaining access. Secondly, there can be no guarantee that the hacker does not damage the system even if the intention is only to gain access.

Information worth billions of ECU is stored on computing systems and they are being linked increasingly to public or semi-public networks. Clearly, companies' financial data could be of value in planning investments. More seriously, information about an individual person could be used for blackmail. Thus, the theft of information can be a profitable crime and should be the subject of legislation quite apart from legislation relating to the subsequent crime.

The problems of detection, identification of the criminal, the collection of evidence and the presentation of evidence in court present almost insuperable difficulties to law enforcement authorities. Detection is difficult if no changes are made to data or programs. The only sure method of detection is by logging (and analysing!) every transaction on the system. Identification poses problems since the perpetrator may be a long distance from the scene of the offence — in another country or even on another continent — and can use anonymous public communications facilities. Collection of evidence is related to detection, and the presentation of any evidence often requires expert witnesses to explain complex technical issues in terms that are comprehensible to non-technical judges and juries.

UNAUTHORISED INTERCEPTION

This is defined as:

> The interception, made without right and by technical means of communications to, from and within a computer system or network."

This can be considered as a new kind of wire-tapping. The offence concerns a situation where the offender takes the data as they are. The communication can take place inside a single computer system, between two computer systems belonging to the same person, two computers communicating with one another, or between a computer and a person.

UNAUTHORISED REPRODUCTION OF A PROTECTED COMPUTER PROGRAM

The report defines this as:

> "The reproduction, distribution or communication to the public without right of a computer program which is protected by law."

Software theft accounts for the largest number of all computer-related crimes. Patent law is only applicable, to a limited extent, to the technical side of computer programs. Trade secret law does not apply to non-secret programs and generally cannot be used against third parties who acquire the secret in good faith.

Most industrialised countries now give programs the additional possibility of copyright protection by extensive interpretation of existing law, express amendments or specific acts. The protectable subject matter is not the mathematical or technical idea, but rather its embodiment in a recorded program. Generally, source and object codes are capable of copyright protection. Even the loading of a program from an external carrier into the internal memory of the computer may be considered as copying in terms of copyright law.

COMMISSION DIRECTIVE

A Council Directive on the Legal Protection of Computer Programs was published on 12 April 1989. The proposed Directive would require Member States to protect computer programs as literary works, subject to special provisions which would limit the scope of protection for certain aspects of programs. In particular, protection would not extend to 'the ideas, principles, logic, algorithms or programming languages underlying the program'. Moreoever, ('where the specification of interfaces constitutes ideas and principles which underlie the program, those ideas and principles are not copyrightable subject matter') (Article 1.3). These limitations on the scope of protection to be given are indicative of the Commission's sensitivity to the possibility that the grant of broad exclusive rights might tend to promote anti-competitive behaviour on the part of rights owners. It is interesting that the Commission took the unusual step of publishing, with the proposed Directive, both a detailed Explanatory Memorandum and a note of its conclusions on the anti-trust implications of the Directive.

Restrictive acts

Article 4 of the proposed Directive provides, "Subject to the provisions of Article 5, the exclusive rights referred to in Article 1 shall include the right to authorise:

(a) the reproduction of a computer program by any means and in any form, in part or in whole. Insofar as they necessitate a reproduction of the program in whole, loading, viewing, running, transmission or storage of the computer program shall be considered restrictive acts;

(b) the adaptation of a computer program;

(c) the distribution of a computer program by means of sale, licensing, lease, rental and the importation for these purposes.

"The right to control the distribution of a program shall be exhausted in respect of its sale and its importation following the first marketing of the program by the rightholder or with his consent."

The Article 4(a) restrictions on reproduction in the course of loading, viewing, running, transmission or storage of a program, will confirm the fundamental basis for software licensing. There is no equivalent elaboration of the term 'adaptation'. Note also the specific statement in Article 4(c) of the 'exhaustion of rights' doctrine. As currently drafted, the reference is to distribution of a program. It is to be hoped that this will either be changed or will be interpreted to mean a copy of a program rather than the program itself.

LIKELY IMPACT ON SOFTWARE DISTRIBUTION

Even more worrying for the software owners and distributors are the 'exceptions to the restricted acts' set out in Article 5 of the proposed Directive:

"1. Where a computer program has been sold or made available to the public other than by a written Licence agreement signed by both parties, the acts enumerated in Article 4(a) and (b) shall not require the authorisation of the rightholder, insofar as they are necessary for the use of the program. Reproduction and adaptation of the program other than for the purposes of its use shall require the authorisation of the rightholder.

2. Where a computer program has been sold or made available to the public by means other than a written licence agreement signed by both parties, the exclusive right of the rightholder to authorise rental shall not be used to prevent use of the program by the public in non-profit making public libraries."

If implemented in its present form, Article 5.1 might substantially undermine widely-used structures for mass-market distribution of software packages. A great deal of software is 'made available to the public other than by a written licence agreement signed by both parties'. For example, shrink-wrapped packages are frequently supplied to end-users in circumstances where it is not feasible to obtain signed user registration cards. Article 5.1 would appear to permit anyone with a lawfully obtained copy of such a package to put it on a network and allow an unlimited number of users access to it without obtaining permission from or making payment to the copyright owner. This might be the end of site licensing, and would undermine further the industry's confidence, already justifiably shaky, in the efficacy of shrink-wrap licensing.

Likely Impact on Bespoke Software Developers

A notable provision of the proposed Directive states that "where a computer program is created under a contract, the natural or legal person who commissioned the program shall be entitled to exercise all rights in respect of the program, unless otherwise provided by contract". In other words, the customer will own bespoke software, not the software house. This reverses the position under UK and virtually every other copyright law and, if it survives in its present form, will represent a trap for the unwary software house.

Parliamentary Discussion

A Bill, based on the Directive and aimed at strengthening legal protection of computer programs and making it uniform throughout the Community, had a lively first reading in the European Parliament in Summer 1990. Of the 57 amendments proposed to the subsequent Bill — "the result of an unprecedented degree of lobbying, mostly by multinationals" — complained one MEP, 15 were adopted.

The explanation, according to the European Parliament's Committee on Legal Affairs and Citizen's Rights which is principally charged with proposing amendments to the Commission's draft BIll, is that it is "a relatively new field for which even leading countries such as the USA, Japan, Germany, France, or the UK have not come up with entirely clear and unequivocal solutions on the complex points of reverse engineering and the moral rights of the author".

The Commission's draft, strangely for a body that maintains an 'Open Systems' stance, leaned towards giving the author all the rights over interface details. This is in contradiction to normal practice, and to case law where it exists, and suited SAGE (Software Action Group for Europe) whose members include IBM, DEC, Apple and Siemens, and whose fears include piracy. Similar views are held by the Business Software Alliance representing six large US publishers of software for personal computers.

Facing the other way, ECIS (European Committee for Interoperable Systems) wants Community law to allow interfaces to be studied. Its members include Amdahl, Bull, Fujitsu, NCR and Unisys, as well as small European computer companies. Large user companies have also banded together to form the Computer Users of Europe (CUE) to lend their weight to the case for permitting access to interface code so that they can connect together equipment from a variety of suppliers. Members of CUE include Barclays Bank, Galileo International, the German Aerospace Centre DLR, W H Smith and BUPA.

The Legal Affairs Committee, inclining more towards ECIS and CUE views, stated that it wanted to "open up this area, with the clear purpose of allowing the interoperability of systems and thus helping to create more computer programmes and increase the creativity of programmes produced by either individuals or groups of persons, or businesses, especially small or medium-sized ones, without forgetting the growing needs and difficulties of users and whilst preventing the software market from becoming totally dominated by powerful hardware companies."

A minority of Legal Affairs Committee was fundamentally opposed, holding that creativity would go out of the window if copying were made so easy.

During the debate, Commissioner Martin Bangemann partially adjusted the Commission's position in saying he was prepared to accept the principle behind the key amendments on interfaces and interoperability.

The other two Committees of the European Parliament involved in reviewing the Commission's draft had other concerns. The Energy, Research and Technology Committee was worried about the strain being placed on normal copyright principles by the attempt to fit computer programs in. The Economic and Monetary Affairs and Industrial Policy Committee, on the other hand, felt that the widespread observance of copyright principles outweighed any uncertainty in their applicability to software. The main problem is that ideas are not protected by normal copyright legislation. It is the expression of those ideas that is protected.

The amendments adopted by the European Parliament included:

—   specific reference to the Berne Convention for protection of literary and artistic works (this is continually updated and has been ratified by 89 countries);

—   definition of a computer program, even while recognising that the Commission had not wanted to give an autonomous definition where there is no widely recognised one;

—   an extended definition of program authorship to include legal as well as natural persons;

—   restriction of the rights of the employer over programs to economic ones;

—   allowing acts essential to the creation or operation of interoperable programs with permission;

—   copyright for 50 years from the beginning of the year following publication of the program or, where the program is not published, its creation;

—   inserting 1 January 1993 as the starting date for member state implementation of any new laws;

— making the Directive applicable also to programs created prior to 1 January 1993;

— setting up a consultative committee, including associations representing program authors, to monitor implementation problems and to suggest improvements.

Now it is up to the Commission to amend the draft legislation in accordance with the wishes of the Parliament. It appears that the Commission would be prepared to permit decompilation of a program subject to certain restrictions:

— the information needed from the program is not published or available elsewhere;

— the developer looks at only the necessary areas of the program;

— any information obtained must not be passed on to a third party;

— the information must not be used to make a rival product.

If the Commission makes substantial modifications to the draft, there will be more opportunity for lobbying before it goes back to the full European Parliament for a second reading.

UNAUTHORISED REPRODUCTION OF A TOPOGRAPHY

With reference to the design of printed circuit boards, the report considered:

> "The reproduction without right of a topography, protected by law, of a semiconductor product, or the commercial exploitation or the importation for that purpose, done without right, of a topography or of a semiconductor product manufactured by using the topography."

In most countries, protection by copyright, patent, trademark, trade secret and unfair competition law is considered incomplete or at least as being unclear in its scope of application to this offence.

A Council of Ministers Directive of 16 December, 1986 has been transformed into national law in several Member States and will be in others. Similar activity has taken place in EFTA countries.

This Directive, as well as national acts, contains important exceptions which limit the offence to clear cases of piracy, eg exceptions include private reproduction for non-commercial aims, for teaching and for research, and 'reverse engineering' for the purpose of creating a competing topography.

AN OPTIONAL LIST OF COMPUTER CRIMES

The report also listed crimes on which there was no consensus for action. These will be formulated for legislation after further discussion, and lobbying, within the Community.

Alteration of computer data or programs

"The alteration of computer data or computer programs without right" which distinguishes 'alteration' from 'erasure, damage, deterioration and suppression of data' (see above). This has been the subject of legislation in a number of countries. the alteration changes the informational quality of data or programs, usually advantageously, eg infringement of, or interference with, the right of disposal of the data or the infringement of privacy. Examples are the addition of new data or combination with other data.

Computer espionage

"The acquisition by improper means or the disclosure, transfer or use of a trade or commercial secret without right or any other legal justification, with intent either to cause economic loss to the person entitled to the secret or to obtain an unlawful economic advantage for oneself or a third person."

Patent, copyright, design patent and trademark law and existing criminal laws are inadequate. With the introduction of the computer, the ease of misappropriation, combined with the potentially enormous value of a compact body of information, has added immensely to the incentives for industrial espionage. On the other hand, the usefulness of a free flow of information puts limits on the protection of trade secrets. Too extensive protection might impair the mobility and the professional advancement of employees.

Unauthorised use of a computer

"The use of a computer system or network without right, that either:

(a)   is made by the acceptance of a significant risk of loss being caused to the person entitled to use the system or harm to the system or its functioning, or

(b)   is made with the intent to cause loss to the person entitled to use the system or harm to the system or its functioning, or

(c)   causes loss to the person entitled to use the system or harm to the system or its functioning."

The three phrases, a to c, are alternatives. Known cases of this offence are rare but the number of unreported cases is estimated to be rather high. Employees, staff and students have been the main offenders. Most of the offences are trivial but there may be cases causing considerable economic harm. Security measures and contractual or disciplinary law remedies are important. Punishment in connection with this offence should be a last resort.

The majority of Council of Europe members believe the mere unlawful use of a computer deserves no punishment, especially when there is no real, immediate danger of harm or damage.

Unauthorised use of a protected computer program

"The use without right of a computer program which is

protected by law and which has been reproduced without right, with the intent either to procure an unlawful economic gain for himself or for another person or to cause harm to the holder of the right."

This is akin to reading a book that has been printed in infringement of copyright or listening to a tape with music which is copied illegally but the danger of economic loss caused by this offence is much higher. The aim of the proposal is to supplement the penal protection of programs that are amenable to copyright.

DATA PROTECTION

The Council of Europe produced a Convention, in 1981, on data protection which protects the individual against abuses related to data collection and processing whilst permitting the free flow of information, including that across national borders. The Convention has been ratified by ten of the Council's 23 members, including seven within the Community, and also by some countries that are not members.

The Commission has submitted a Communication to the European Council which contains six proposals:

1. A Directive aimed at establishing a high level of protection throughout the Community which will be based on the above Convention and recent legislative developments. Seven member states (Denmark, France, Germany, Ireland, Luxembourg, the Netherlands and the UK) have differing national legislation. The Commission would like to extend the protection of data to member states at present without legislation and also ensure a uniformly high standard;

2. A recommendation in favour of negotiations for the Community to adhere to the above Convention, thereby allowing official contacts with countries outside the Community;

3. A resolution to extend protection to any kind of data contained in public sector files which do not fall within the scope of Community law;

4.   A declaration applying the same protection principles to personal data held by Community institutions and bodies;

5.   A Directive specifically tackling the problem of bringing a homogeneous and high level of protection in the case of expanding telecommunications such as ISDN mobile services;

6.   A decision concerning the security of information systems which includes an action plan.

The Commission is looking ahead to the post-1992 era when improved informatics systems will make it difficult for an individual to keep track of data being stored and communicated around the Community. The Commission proposes, therefore, to make it illegal for personal data of any kind to be stored or transferred without an individual's knowledge and agreement.

DIRECTIVE ON VISUAL DISPLAY UNITS

As an example of the detailed level of work undertaken by the Commission in connection with legislation for health and safety. I can cite the Directive on minimum health and safety requirements for work with visual display screen equipment which was adopted by the Council of Ministers in June 1990.

Member states have until the end of 1992 to implement the following measures:

—   employers to analyse display screen workstations to evaluate safety and health conditions, taking appropriate measures to remedy any risks found;

—   employers to ensure workstations entering service after 31 December 1992 meet the requirements contained in the annex to the Directive which sets standards for display screens, keyboards, furniture, lighting, working environment, task design and software;

—   employers to ensure that workstations in service before 31 December 1992 are adapted to comply with the requirements in the annex within four years of that date;

— employers to provide for workers to receive information and training, and for consultation and participation of workers and/or their representatives;

— employers to plan activities so that daily work on a display screen is periodically interrupted by breaks or changes of activity;

— workers to be entitled to an eye and eyesight test before starting display screen work, at regular intervals thereafter and if they experience visual difficulties. Workers will also be entitled to an ophthalmological examination if the eye test shows this to be necessary; and they must be provided with special spectacles if these are needed for their work, where normal ones cannot be used.

8 Professionalism

INTRODUCTION

There are a variety of bodies that exist to forward the interests of the professional informatics workers of Europe. Some are purely 'learned societies', open to all, with no aspirations to be professional bodies. At the other extreme, there are a few elite societies, highly restrictive in their membership, normally treating the IT profession as a branch of engineering. In between, there are a variety of bodies with a mixture of objectives, learned society, professional society, registration body, informatics members club, etc. The British Computer Society (BCS) with its 31,000 members is typical of these. Founded in 1957, it has been a body providing journals and meetings for its members. For the past six years it has operated under a Royal Charter, and so now is under a duty deriving from this to pursue the interests of the profession it represents, both for and in the interests of its members, and on behalf of the British community at large. It is also affiliated to the UK's Engineering Council so that suitably qualified members can register as professional engineers.

In France the equivalent societies are AFIN and AFGET, in Germany GI, in the Netherlands NGI, in Italy AICA, in Denmark DANFIP, in Spain LESCO, and in Switzerland SSIII. There are various other societies in these countries and others of the community. In most countries it is clear enough which is the leading professional body, but sometimes it is not easy to choose, though IFIP has done so by restricting membership to one per country. The societies of Europe have now agreed to work together and have formed the Council of European Professional

Informatics Societies (CEPIS) to help all informatics professionals in Europe. Under the umbrella of the regular six-monthly meetings various working groups have been, and will be, established to examine specific issues. Chief amongst these is the matter of professionalism and the equivalence of qualifications. Another that has been established covers legal aspects, such as the problems of confidentiality, hacking, and intellectual property rights. Others will be looking at professional development and training, at publications and conferences, and probably at matters of concern to the Commission, of the member governments and of individual European firms to help progress some of these issues. At present, the secretariat of the Federation is based in the BCS in London. The BCS is proposing to move its offices out of London but the current address is:

> The British Computer Society
> 13 Mansfield Street
> LONDON W1M 0BP, UK
>
> Telephone: 071 637 0471 or + 44 71 637 0471.

The reasons for the European informatics societies collaborating are:

— to identify how informatics systems can be used to provide an infrastructure for pan-European trading, social co-operation and other purposes;

— to ensure that the skills needed are available to enable the Community to use informatics to pursue its economic and social objectives;

— to provide information to politicians and other policy makers on the benefits to be gained from the use of informatics;

— to improve the competence and standing of workers in the informatics professions;

— to determine a uniform approach in dealing with the rest of the world — Eastern Europe, developing countries etc.

Clearly, the pursuit of Open Systems supports these objectives, and the cause is helped by the concerted effort of all the societies working together. Other areas in which '12 heads are better than one' include defining a code of professional conduct and determining educational and training requirements, particularly bearing in mind the rapid rate of change in technology with the consequent need for updating professional skills.

PROFESSIONAL QUALIFICATIONS ACROSS EUROPE

The Treaty of Rome recognised that a fundamental goal for Europe was the free movement of workers at all levels of qualification, but particularly at the professional level. The reasons for encouraging mobility of workers are that they have a wider choice of appointments, they can choose the best conditions of appointment — which in turn results in a general improvement of conditions throughout the Community — and skills can be directed to areas where they are most needed. Specific Directives have been hammered out over the years for professions, such as those of doctors, nurses, dentists, veterinary surgeons, midwives, pharmacists and architects. CEPIS is ensuring that attention is now being focused on the free movement of informatics professionals.

A general Council Directive was adopted by the Community in 1989 covering the mutual recognition of "higher education diplomas awarded on completion of vocational courses of at least three years duration". The intention is that the diplomas of another member state will be recognised, provided that certain conditions are met, without going through lengthy procedures prior to harmonisation of courses.

Though aimed at recognition for professional purposes, it is sure to have a wider impact, for example, on the mutual recognition of academic qualifications. For higher education qualifications there are various unilateral, bilateral and multilateral conventions between member states.

Since 1984 a network of National Academic Recognition Information Centres (NARIC) has existed, but the mobility at student level in the Community is still small. For the UK the number of post-graduate students going to the USA still vastly outnumbers those going to study or work on the Continent. Overall student mobility within the Community is less than one per cent of the total number of students in higher education. The Commission's ERASMUS scheme aims to increase significantly the number of students going to study in other countries of the Community.

The Joint Study Programme (JSP) scheme and the Short Study Visit (SSV) schemes have existed in the Community for many years. The JSP scheme encourages exchange of higher educational establishment staff and joint curriculum development. Both the JSP and SSV schemes have been structured to encourage mutual recognition of qualifications. the NARIC network staff can receive grants under the SSV scheme to make visits to look at national recognition problems on the ground. Now the ERASMUS scheme aims to increase mobility to at least ten per cent of the total higher education student population by 1992.

Mutual academic recognition is central to the whole ERASMUS process, which was approved by the Council in June 1987. The existing JSP and SSV schemes have illustrated the way in which such schemes serve to accelerate the mutual recognition of qualifications. As a result, it is reasonable to expect that the ERASMUS programme, which will commit a budget of ECU 175 million over the three years 1987, 1988, and 1989 in what is seen as the first stage of a rolling programme, will improve the situation on the mutual recognition of qualifications in Europe. Since the problem of mutual academic recognition lies at the heart of the mutual recognition of professional qualifications and status in Europe, solution of the problem is critical.

Before looking at the movement of people that may migrate across Europe after professional qualifications have been harmonised, it is important to recognise that programmes to encourage mobility of the student level, like ERASMUS, are not the only mechanism for encouraging mobility. The Community's research programmes, for example, may be a more potent force for encouraging mobility because they impact directly on the workforce — admittedly the rather untypical R&D workforce — of Europe's industries.

THE PROFESSIONAL CHALLENGES

Since informatics is now involved in, and influences, most human, industrial, commercial and social activities, the informatics professionals are having to stand up and defend their standards and profession. The challenges stem basically from three causes:

1. The responsibility for safety-critical and secure software;

2. The problems generated by the hacker and the virus generator;

3. The dangers of biases in inference computing.

Because we are at last within sight of being able to check that software meets set specifications through logical formal methods, society is becoming more aware of the dangers to human life posed by errors in informatics systems that control certain equipment such as 'fly-by-wire' aircraft and power stations. Similar problems arise for the security of systems where financial fraud is a challenge, or the dangers of unauthorised access to personal information stored in databases. In the end, as with other branches of engineering, there is only one way of satisfying society that every reasonable step has been taken in producing the system to ensure against faults and security lapses — that is to place the responsibility in the hands of responsible professional experts. In the UK that means chartered engineers where their professional body will vouch for their professionalism. In other countries of Europe it means an engineer licensed by the state in one way or another.

The responsible engineer has to 'sign off' the system, and to face a court hearing if things should go wrong. The court will wish to see that the responsible engineer has adopted the 'best' approaches, and has checked that the team are well-trained and taking up-to-date precautions. It is the duty of the professional society to ensure that the engineers, to whom they ascribe professional status, do meet the standards they propose and maintain. In addition, the professional society must be prepared to strike out of membership those of its members who do not maintain the approved standards.

In applying these procedures to informatics, various bodies are working on draft documents. In the UK the Ministry of Defence has taken the lead, and the Health and Safety Executive is not far behind. In Europe the Commission has working parties examining the matter. It is now only a matter of time before the informatics professional has to take real responsibilty, in a legal sense, for his systems. The problems of hacking and virus propagation are moral rather than professional issues, but professionals and their societies have to take a stand. The expert hacker inevitably extracts some admiration from the professional who can appreciate the expertise, just as the master safe cracker extracts some admiration from the safe maker. But they are both criminals nonetheless, and the informatics professionals and their professional societies have to make that clear. Society expects protection from criminals; equally it expects its informatics experts to protect it against the hacker.

The third challenge to the informatics professional comes from inference computing. With conventional computing, from which the vast majority of applications are derived, the result of a computer run is likely to be based on the certainties of the laws of mathematics or of Boolean logic. In these circumstances there is little scope for bias in the results. But with inference computing, such as expert systems and knowledge-based systems, the situation is different. The rule base will never be complete, the input data may be incorrect or incomplete, the meta-knowledge that controls the inference process may be incorrect or incomplete. The results obtained from such computation may be correct, but can never be regarded as totally reliable. Such systems are open to bias by selection of the rules and knowledge. The dangers are obvious when one remembers that the user public has come to expect computers to give the 'right answer'. Commercial, political, even religious, influences may result in bias. This is, of course, commonplace — just consider the selective advice to doctors designed to persuade them to prescribe a particular type of drug. But the added danger with inference computing is partly that users do not expect bias in computer systems, and partly that expert systems make knowledge accessible to a wider public than would arise for the same information in printed form.

It could be argued that such matters of bias are nothing to do with the informatics professional who builds the system. But society will be right not to accept that, and to expect the professionals, at the very least, to warn the relevent authority when they believe that dangerous bias is being introduced into systems for which they have some responsibility.

THE PROFESSIONAL SOCIETY IN EUROPE

The challenges to the professional societies of Europe are clear. They must create codes of conduct for their members, propagate them, and police and enforce them. Europe is becoming such a small world that there is no place for a variety of codes and standards. Mobility of professionals will require that they operate to the same standards across Europe. This implies that the societies of Europe have to get together to agree these codes. This will not be easy, for differences in culture and law have to be overcome. But, just as the societies are making progress on reciprocal recognition of qualifications, so they will have to strive to produce common codes of professional practice. The public will expect and, indeed, demand it of them.

The strengthening of the European industrial base cannot rely solely on actions defined in Brussels, but will require co-ordinated actions on the part of politicians, industrialists and educators. Technological innovation and rapid technology transfer into the profit making sectors of industry will be two of the key elements in determining the future health of European Information Technology and Telecommunications industries. Clearly, the professional institutions, and professional engineers, have a major role to play in this area.

Professional societies should also unite to give advice to policy makers on the need for more support for research and development in the appropriate technologies, and for improved education in informatics. This, of course, directly impacts on the societies' responsibilities to work with academic institutions regarding course content and also with industry to ensure that the appropriate training actions are being covered. This is a particularly important issue since it is not clear that we have the mechanisms capable of reacting sufficiently quickly to the rate of change of technology in informatics and telecommuni-cations.

Looking ahead into future exploitation of new technology professional societies should take an independent view of the technological innovations that are likely to shape the informatics and telecommunications product lines of the future. They can take an industry-wide view. In many instances, company, or even national, perspectives are too parochial to address the real long-term issues.

Glossary of Acronyms, Programmes and Organisations

AFNOR	Association Francaise de Normalisation
AI	Artificial Intelligence
AIM	Advanced Informatics in Medicine in Europe
AIST	Agency of Industrial Science and Technology
Alvey	A UK programme of collaborative research projects between industry and universities, with the Government providing enabling grants, following the recommendations of a committee chaired by John Alvey. The programme ran from 1982 until 1987
ANA	Article Numbering Association
ANSI	American National Standards Institute
AOWS	Asian and Oceanic Workshop
APACS	Association for Payment Clearing Services
ATM	Asynchronous Transfer Mode
Atmosphere	Advanced Tools and Methods for System Production in Heterogeneous Extensible Real Environments — an ESPRIT project
BABT	British Approvals Board for Telecommunications
BACS	Banker's Automated Clearing Service
BC-NET	Business Co-operation NETwork
BEAB	British Electrotechnical Approval Board
BEUC	Bureau of European Consumers Union
BRITE	A Community R&D programme called Basic Research in Industrial Technology for Europe
BSI	British Standards Institution
BSR	Board of Standards Review

CAD	Computer Aided Design
CAM	Computer Aided Manufacture
CBEMA	Computer and Business Equipment Manufacturers Association
CCIR	International Radio Consultative Committee
CCITT	International Telegraph and Telephone Consultative Committee
CCTA	Central Computer and Telecommunications Agency
CEC	Commission of the European Communities, the administration set up in Brussels to pursue the integration of the European community
CEN	European Committee for Standardisation
CENELEC	European Committee for Electrotechnical Standardisation
CEPT	European Conference of Postal and Telecommunications Administrations in Europe
CGS	Cap-Gemini-Sogetti, a French software house
CIM	Computer Integrated Manufacturing
CNMA	Communications Network for Manufacturing Applications
COCOM	Co-ordinating Committee for Multilateral Export Controls
COMETT	COMmunity action in Education and Training for Technology
COREPER	Permanent Representatives Committee in COST
COS	Corporation for Open Systems
COSINE	Co-operation for Open Systems Networking in Europe
COST	European Co-operation in the Field of Scientific and Technical Research, was set up by EC Council of Ministers in 1971 to promote cross-frontier collaboration in R&D. It has seven other Member States as well as those in the EC.
CPMU	COSINE Programme Management Unit
CREST	Committee for Scientific and Industrial Research, consisting of senior officials from national ministries concerned with science policy
CSO	COST Senior Officials Committee
CTS	Conformance Testing Service

DELTA	Developing European Learning through Techno-logical Advance
DIN	German Standards Institute
DKE	German Electrotechnical Commission
DP	Data Processing
DRIVE	A Community R&D programme called Dedicated Road Infrastructure for VEhicle safety
DTI	Department of Trade and Industry
EC	European Community: Belgium, Denmark, France, Germany, Greece, Ireland, Italy, Luxembourg, Netherlands, Portugal, Spain and the United Kingdom
ECIS	European Committee for Interoperable Systems
ECITC	European Committee for IT Testing and Certification
ECM	European Common Market
ECMA	European Computer Manufacturers' Association
ECU	European Currency Unit, approximately equal to the US dollar
EDI	Electronic Data Interchange
EEC	European Economic Community, same as EC
EFT/POS	Electronic Funds Transfer/Point Of Sale
EFTA	The European Free Trade Association consisting of Austria, Finland, Iceland, Norway, Sweden and Switzerland
EMS	Economic and Monetary System
EMU	Economic and Monetary Union
EMUG	European MAP Users Group
ENS	European Nervous System: a proposed information network for the Community covering all governments' applications for security, finance and health
EP	European Parliament
ERA	Electrical Research Association: a research laboratory in the UK funded by companies providing electrical goods or services
ERASMUS	European Community Action Scheme for Mobility of University Students
ESCB	European System of Central Banks
ESPRIT	European Strategic Programme for Research and development in Information Technology

ESSI	European Systems and Software Initiative
ETCOM	European Testing and Conformance of Office and Manufacturing committee
ETSI	European Telecommunications Standards Institute
EUREKA	A general European R&D programme involving the countries in EFTA as well as the Community
EHTP	European High Technology Programme
EVCA	European Venture Capital Association
EWOS	European Workshop for Open Systems
FDDI	Fibre Distributed Data Interchange
FIPS	Federal Information Processing Standards
FRAMEWORK	The name of the Community's overall research programme
GATT	General Agreement for Tariffs and Trade
GDP	Gross Domestic Product
GEIS	General Electric Information Services
GOSIP	Government Open Systems Interconnect Profile
GUS	Guide to Use of Standards
HDTV	High Definition TeleVision
HUFIT	HUman Factors laboratories in Information Technology: an ESPRIT project
IBC	Integrated Broadband Communication
IC	Integrated Circuit
IEC	International Electrotechnical Committee
IEE	Institution of Electrical Engineers
IEEE	Institute of Electrical and Electronic Engineers
Informatics	A term used widely throughout Europe (albeit with variations on the last few letters) for computing, information processing and data communications
IGC	Inter-Governmental Conference
INSTAC	INformation technology research & STAndardisation Centre
IPSJ	Information Processing Society of Japan
ISDN	Integrated Services Digital Network
ISO	International Standards Organisation
ISP	International Standards Profile

IT	Information Technology
ITAEGM	IT Advisory Expert Group on advanced Manufacturing technology
ITAEGS	IT Advisory Expert Group for co-ordinated planning of open systems functional Standards
ITAEGT	IT Advisory (and co-ordination) Experts Group for private Telecommunications networks
ITSTC	Information Technology STandardisation steering Committee
ITU	International Telecommunications Union
ITUSA	Information Technology Users' Standards Association
JBMA	Japan Business machine Makers' Association
JEIDA	Japan Electronic Industry Development Association
JESSI	Joint European Sub-micron Silicon Initiative
JICA	Japanese International Co-operation Agency
JISC	Japanese Industrial Standards Committee
JSA	Japanese Standards Association
JSP	Joint Study Programme
JST	Joint STudy programme, to exchange staff between higher education institutions and develop joint curricula
JTC1 (SWG-SP)	Joint Technical Committee 1 (Special Working Group for Strategic Planning)
LAMSAC	Local Authority Management Services and Computing Committee in the UK
LAN	Local Area Network
LEO	Lyon's Electronic Office
MAP	Manufacturing Application Protocol
Megachip	A project to manufacture a silicon chip with a million gates
MFLOPS	A Million Floating point OPerations per Second, used to compare the power of computers
MITI	Japan's Ministry of International Trade and Industry
MMI	Man Machine Interface
MOTIS	Message Orientated Text Interchange Systems
MOD	Ministry of Defence in the UK

NARIC   National Academic Recognition Information
                Centre
NBS   National Bureau of Standards (see NIST)
NCC   The UK's National Computing Centre
NCTL   National Computer and Telecommunications
                Laboratory
NI   Nationalised Industries
NIST   The USA's National Institute of Standards
                Technology (formerly NBS)
NRDC   National Research Development Corporation: an
                organisation set up by the UK Government to
                encourage, and sometimes finance, the
                development of saleable commodities from bright
                ideas

OASIS   Organisation And Systems InnovationS Ltd
ODA   Office Document Architecture
OECD   Organisation for Economic Co-operation and
                Development
OFTEL   OFfice of TELecommunications
OSF   Open Systems Foundation
OSI   Open Systems Interconnection
OSITOP   OSI Technical and Office Protocols
OSTC   Open Systems Testing Corporation

PC   Personal Computer
PCTE   Portable Common (software) Tools Environment
PEIN   Plan Electrónico e Informático Nacional, Spain's
                programme for developing its IT industry
PICKUP   Professional Industrial Commercial Keep Up-to-
                date Programme
POSI   Promoting conference for Open Systems
                Interconnection
PTT   National authority for postal, telephone and
                telecommunication services
PROMETHEUS PROgramme for European Traffic with Highest
                Efficiency and Unprecedented Safety — a project
                in EUREKA
PROTEAS   PROTotypes European Access System

RACE   Research and development in Advanced
                Communications technologies in Europe

R&D	Research and Development
RARE	Reseaux Associes pur la Recherche Europeene
RTI	Road Transport Informatics
SAD	Single Administrative Document
SAGE	Software Action Group for Europe
SATRA	Shoes and Allied Trades Research Association: a research laboratory in the UK funded by companies in shoe and allied trades
SINGLE EUROPEAN ACT (1986)	Signed by governments of all EC countries to provide reforms in the law-making process to speed up decision making whilst preparing the framework for EC policies
SIS	Swedish Information technology Standards institute
SITPRO	Simplification of International Trade PROcedures board
SME	Small and Medium sized Enterprises
SOGITS	Senior Officials Group: Information Technology Standardisation
SOGT	Senior Officials Group: Telecommunications
SPAG	Standards Promotion Application Group
SPRINT	Strategic PRogramme for INnovation and Technology transfer
SSV	Short Study Visit, for the purpose of examining the problem of mutual recognition of qualifications
SWIFT	Society of World Inter-banking Financial Telecommunications
TAG	Technical Advisory Group
TAPC	Telecommunications Attachment Policy Committee
TED	Tenders Electronic Daily, a database of public procurements throughout the EC
TEDIS	Trade Electronic Data Interchange Service
TII	Technology Innovation Information: a European association for the transfer of technology innovation and industrial information
TIP	Technology Integration Project (for faster application of the results of R&D)

TOP	Technical and Office Protocol
TRAC	Technical Recommendations Applications Committee
UETP	University Enterprise Training Partnership
UNICORN	United Nations Interactive Concept Over Reservation Network
UTE	Union Technique de l'Electricity
VADS	Value Added Data Services
VAT	Value Added Tax
VLSI	Very Large Scale Integration, a large number of gates or memory on a silicon chip
4GL	Fourth Generation Language

Bibliography

Serial Publications

IT in Europe, 10 per year, A Plus Publications, Tithe Barn, Tithe Court, Langley, Berks, SL3 8AS, UK. ISSN 0960-2402, subscription — £185.

Interface Europe, 6 per year, Interface Europe, 142a, The Broadway, Didcot, Oxon, OX11 8RJ, UK. ISSN 0955-4890, subscription — £85.

New European, 4 per year, New European Publications, 14/16 Carroun Road, Vauxhall, London, SW8 1JT, UK. ISSN 0953-1432, subscription — £20.

Books

Cecchini P, *The European Challenge — 1992*, Wildwood House Ltd. — £7.95. ISBN 0-7045-0613-0 (1988, 1989, 1990).

Clifford Chance (Lawyers), *1992: An Introductory Guide (Second Edition 1990)* and *Information Technology 1992 (1990)*, Clifford Chance Publications Unit, Royex House, Aldermanbury Square, London EC2V 7LD, UK. Free of charge.

Drew J, *Europe 1992: Developing an Active Company Approach to the European Market*. Published for the Commission of the European Communities by Whurr Publishers Ltd. — £5 (1988).

Dudley J W, *1992 — Strategies for the Single Market*, Kogan Page Ltd. — £10.95. ISBN 0-7494-0012-9 (Second Edition 1990).

Owen R, and Dynes M, *The Times Guide to 1992*, Times Books Ltd. — £5.95. ISBN 0-7230-0316-5 (1989).

Index

access, unauthorised	133
A Plus Publications	39
Aeritalia	70
AFGET	147
AFIN	147
AICA	147
AIM	38, 66, 80
ALVEY Programme	24
Amdahl	17, 139
ANA	46, 47
Apple	17, 22, 139
Apricot	18
Article Numbering Association	see ANA
ASCII	119
ATM	77
AT&T	75, 116
audit, European	36, 40
BACS	47
Bangemann, Martin	13, 139
Bankers Automated Clearing Service	see BACS
Barclays Bank	49, 139
BC-NET	35, 59, 60
Beregovoy, Pierre	13
Berne Convention	140
BMW	70
Bouhu, Professor	53
BRITE	70
British Aerospace	70

British Computer Society   8, 147, 148
British Electrotechnical Approval Board   11
British Standards Institution   11, 43, 128
Bull   22, 117, 139
BUPA   139
Bureau of European Consumer Unions   10
Business Software Alliance   139

CAD   65, 68, 79
CAM   65
CAP   see Intro
CAP-Gemini-Sogetti   see CGS
Carpentier, Michel   19
CCIR   109
CCITT   109, 114, 121
CCTA   114, 116
Cecchini, Paolo   38
Celex   39
CEN   43, 75, 109, 110, 112,
                                                  122, 138
CENELEC   43, 75, 109, 110, 122
                                                  128
CEPIS   148
CEPT   29, 43, 128
CGS   see Intro, 25, 27
change, technological   see Intro
Christopherson, Henning   13
CIM   70
CNMA   70
Cockfield, Lord   2
COCOM   17
Collison, Ian   73
COMECON   16
COMETT   91-97
Commission of the European   2-6, 14, 18,
   Communities   19, 20, 41, 42
Common Agricultural Policy   1, 6
common European home   16
Company Statute   13
competitiveness   see Intro, 35-59
conduct, professional   149, 151, 153
CONS   121

contract law   43
Control Data (CDC)   22
copying, unauthorised   135
copyright   135-144, 148
COREPER   3
COS   127
COSINE   123-126
COST   82, 83
Council of Europe   4, 129, 143, 144
Council of Ministers   2, 4, 5, 6, 9
CPMU   124
crime, computer related   129-145
CSMA/CD   121, 122
CSO   82
CTS   112
CUE   139

damage, computer   132
DANFIP   147
data protection   4, 39, 144
Datamation   21
Delors, Jacques   2, 3
DELTA   66, 89, 97-100
Department of Trade and Industry
  (DTI)   36, 42
design   51
development regional   9
DFN   125
DG XII   97
DG XIII   19, 20, 42, 43, 96,
                                      103
Digital (DEC)   17, 22, 116, 140
directives   5, 7, 39, 109-111,
                                      136-142, 144, 145,
                                      149
Directorates General   42
DLR   139
Drew, John   36, 39, 40
DRIVE   38, 66, 81, 82
Duhamel, Michel   59
Dumas, Roland   16
dumping   18

Eastern Europe   see Intro. 16, 18, 148
EBU   75
ECIS   139
ECITC   112, 113
ECMA   69
Economic and Monetary System   12
Economic and Monetary Union   12
Economic Commission for Europe
  (UN)   46
ECU   10
EDI   see Intro. 37, 38, 44,
                                        45-50, 117
EDIFACT   46, 48, 49, 117
EFT   47
EFTA   see Intro. 4, 15, 16,
                                        75, 112
Electronic Data Interchange   see EDI
Electronic Data Systems   47
Electronic Funds Transfer   see EFT
electronic mail   121
ELTA   98
EN   109, 122
Engineering Council (UK)   147
Enterprise initiative   42
ERA   52
ERASMUS   100, 101, 150
ESPRIT   20, 23, 24, 25, 26,
                                        38, 65, 67-73, 84,
                                        106, 112, 114
ESSI   31
ETCOM   113
Ethernet   121
ETSI   29, 75, 127, 128
EUREKA   16, 25, 83, 84, 112,
                                        123
Eurobase   39
European Common Market   2, 5
European Community   1
European Council   2, 83
European Court of Justice   4, 8, 39
European Economic Space   15, 16
European Nervous System   67

European Parliament   3, 4, 5, 9, 15, 41,
                                         138, 140, 141

European Patent Organisation   53
European Social Fund   91
European System of Central Banks   12
European Venture Capital Association   see EVCA
EUROTECNET   88
EUROTRA   103
EVCA   52
EWOS   112, 126-128
exports   19

FAMOS   84
FDDI   121
fibre, optical   77, 78
forgery, computer   132
Framework Programme   61-67, 88
fraud, computer   131
Fujitsu   18, 22, 26, 35, 139

Galileo International   139
GATT   19
GEIS   47
General Electric Information Services   see GEIS
General Motors   47, 70
GI   147
Goldstar   26
GOSIP   108
GUS   127

harmonisation   11, 32, 110, 112, 127,
                                         130, 131
HDTV   66, 78, 84
Health and Safety Executive (UK)   152
Hewlett-Packard   22
Hitachi   22, 26

IBC   30, 74-79
IBM   17, 22, 75, 116, 140
ICL   18, 22, 35, 117
IEC   109
inference computing   151, 152

IFIP   147
Inmos   25
innovation   19, 50, 55-58
'Innovation and Technology Transfer'   55
interception, unauthorised   135
IOP   127
IPSE   69
INS   47, 48
Intel   26
Inter-Governmental Conference   13
'Interface Europe'   39
International Network Services   see INS
IRDS   116
Iron and Steel Community   1
ISDN   32, 74, 75, 98, 145
ISO   69, 109, 114, 117
ISP   127
ITSC   112
IXI   123

JANET   125
Japan   see Intro. 17, 18, 21,
                                               24, 25, 26, 27, 28,
                                               35, 83, 122, 128
JESSI   25, 26
JSP   100, 101, 150
JTCI   109, 128

Kent, A. H.   96
King's College, London   96
Kohl, Chancellor   15
Korea   26, 27

LAN   121, 122
learning, distance   97, 99
legislation   5, 9, 38, 41, 111,
                                               112, 129-146
LESCO   147
levies   18
LINGUA   101, 102
Longman Cartermill   85

man-machine interface   see MMI
MAP   108
market, European   see Intro. 18
marketing   43
Matsushita   26
Megachip project   25
MEI/JVC   26
mergers, cross-border   14, 23, 24
MHS   121
micro-electronics   63, 65, 68, 72, 92, 96
Ministry of Defence (UK)   152
Mitsubishi   21, 26
MMI   69, 72
MOTIS   121
Motorola   26

NARIC   101, 149, 150
National Science Foundation   55
National Standards Institute (USA)   see NSI
NATO   17
NBS-NSI   122
NCR   21, 139
NEC   22, 26
Networkshop   126
NGI   147
Nixdorf   22
NSI (formerly NBS)   46, 122

OASIS   see Intro.
ODA   71, 116, 117
ODETTE   47
office systems   69
Oki   18
Olivetti   22
OMEGA   68
Open Systems   113-128, 140, 149
Open Systems Interconnection   see OSI
OSI   45, 68, 110-128
OSTC   113

Pannenborg, Dr A. E.   71
Pandolfi, Filippo Mariok   20
PATINNOVA '90   53

PCTE	68, 69, 114
peripherals	65, 72
Permanent Representatives Committee	see COREPER
PETE	98
PETRA	103
Philips	22, 25, 26, 71
PICKUP	95
PIMB	69
Plessey	25
political union	13
Portugese Patent Office	54
POSI	122
POSIX	116
printed circuit board	141
procurement, public	7, 29, 44, 45, 106, 110, 111
PROTEAS	84
PTTs	30, 44
qualifications, professional	8, 11, 15, 30, 88, 101, 147, 148-150, 153
RACE	29, 65, 70, 74-79, 112
Rank Xerox	22
RARE	125, 126
Recognition Arrangements	113
recommendations	5, 7
Reference (OSI seven-layer) Model	117-120
Regional Development Fund	43
regulations	5, 28, 32, 39, 110, 129
Round Table	73
sabotage	133
SAGE	140
Samsung	26
Sanyo	26
satellites	77
SATRA	52
science parks	54
SEMA	see Intro.

Sema-metra	See Intro.
semiconductors	25, 26
Shevardnadze, Eduard	16
Siemens	22, 25, 117, 140
Single Administrative Document	44
Single European Act	2,4, 5, 12, 13
Single European Market	10, 12, 36, 37, 40
skills (shortage of)	30, 63, 67, 87, 92
SMEs	8, 9, 35, 51, 59, 60, 88, 91, 96, 99, 139
Smith, W. H.	139
Social Charter	14
societies, professional	147-155
Society for World Inter-bank Financial Telecommunications	see SWIFT
SOFT	98
software	27, 30, 31, 39, 44, 45, 65, 66, 68, 72, 100, 137-141, 151
Sony	26
SPAG	75, 126, 127
Spearhead	40
SPRINT	35, 38, 50-56
SQL	116
SSIII	147
SSV	101, 150
standards	32, 38, 40, 43, 46, 49, 70, 71, 84, 105-128
STC	22
Stock Exchange	48
strategy, business	See Intro. 32, 35, 36
students	8, 10
Supernode machine	68
SURFNET	125
SWIFT	47, 48
switching, circuit	77
switching, packet	77
Technitron	18
TEDIS	50

telecommunications   7, 12, 19, 20, 27-30,
                                      32, 44, 45, 74-76, 83,
                                      84, 99, 110, 117, 125,
                                      127, 145, 153
telephone numbers   see Intro.
TEMPUS   103
Texas Instruments   103
Texas Instruments   26
Thomson   25, 26
TII   35, 52, 55-59
TOP   108
Toshiba   22, 26
TRADACOMS   47
TRADANET   47
transputer   70
Treaty of Rome   1, 4, 5, 149

UETP   92-96
UNICORN   48
Unisys   22, 139
United Nations Interactive Concept
   Over ReservatioN   see UNICORN
University of London   92, 93
UNIX   116
USA   See Intro. 17, 18, 21,
                                      24, 25, 26, 27, 28,
                                      35, 83, 122, 128, 150
USSR   16

VALUE   64
VAT   44
VAX/VMS   116
venture capital   51, 52
visual display units   145
VLSI   68
vote, majority   2

Wang   22
White Paper   40
Wilmot, Robb   see Intro.